BERLITZ®

SCOTLAND

1991/1992 Edition

By the staff of Berlitz Guides

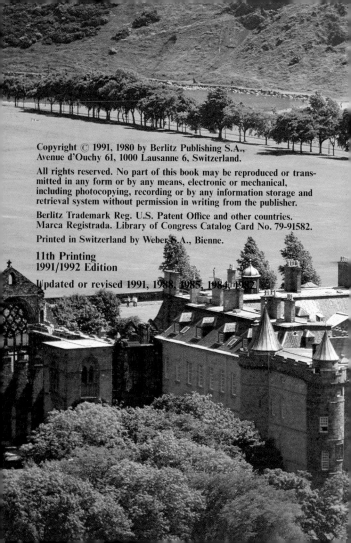

Printed in Switzerland by Weber S.A., Bienne.

11th Printing
1991/1992 Edition

Updated or revised 1991, 1988, 1985, 1984, 1982

How to use our guide

- All the practical information, hints and tips that you will need before and during the trip start on page 102.

- For general background, see the sections Scotland and the Scots, p. 6, and A Brief History, p. 12.

- All the sights to see are listed between pages 23 and 80. Our own choice of sights most highly recommended is pinpointed by the Berlitz traveller symbol.

- Entertainment, nightlife and all other leisure activities are described between pages 82 and 93, while information on restaurants and cuisine is to be found on pages 93 to 100.

- Finally, there is an index at the back of the book, pp. 126–128.

Although we make every effort to ensure the accuracy of all the information in this book, changes occur incessantly. We cannot therefore take responsibility for facts, prices, addresses and circumstances in general that are constantly subject to alteration. Our guides are updated on a regular basis as we reprint, and we are always grateful to readers who let us know of any errors, changes or serious omissions they come across.

Text: Don Larrimore
Photography: Roy Giles
Layout: Doris Haldemann
We're grateful to Dick Fotheringham and Meryl A. Masterton for their help in the preparation of this book. We would also like to thank the Scottish Tourist Board and, in particular, the information centres at Aberdeen, Alloway, Broadford (Skye), Brodick (Arran), Dumfries, Durness, Edinburgh, Fort William and Oban for their considerable assistance.
Cartography: Falk-Verlag, Hamburg

Contents

Photo pp. 2–3; Holyrood Palace

Scotland and the Scots

Deep green glens slicing through majestic mountains, forbidding castles reflected in shimmering lochs, rolling moors awash in the purples of heather or yellows of broom and gorse, sheep dotting every horizon. Scotland with its Highlands, islands and Lowlands is a riot of natural beauty, one of Europe's few remaining wilderness frontiers.

Within easy reach of the cities of Edinburgh, Glasgow, Aberdeen and Dundee are vast tracts of unspoilt country. You might see red deer break cover, golden eagles or even an osprey swoop overhead. In coursing streams magnificent salmon and trout challenge anglers. Seals laze on rocky shores. It's quite possible to tramp all day and not see another human being.

Scotland is a land rich in romantic tradition and stormy history, where clan tartans and skirling bagpipes are not mere tourist gimmicks. The cultural mosaic, like the scenery, is tremendously varied. In Edinburgh, the intellectually and architecturally stimulating capital, they stage a distinguished international festival every summer. Around the country there are plays, concerts, Highland gatherings, folk shows and craft exhibitions. You can visit some 150 of Scotland's 1,200 castles—intact or respectable ruins. Unusual museums, baronial mansions, ancient abbeys, formal gardens and archaeological sites invite exploration. Glasgow has one of Europe's great art galleries. And don't miss the sheepdog trials.

Happily, what you know they say about Scotland's weather isn't always true. Between May and October there are invariably hours and even full days of hot sunshine, interrupting the rain, mist and chill wind which help keep the Scots so hardy. For what it may be worth, Scotland in an average year has as much sun as London. Sightseers and photographers appreciate the amazing visibility on clear days. The grim winters don't daunt skiers, though they aren't much fun in villages isolated by heavy snows.

Covering the northernmost third of the United Kingdom, Scotland—as some natives like

Crab and lobster freshly caught at fishing village of Crail where the welcome's warmer than the weather.

6

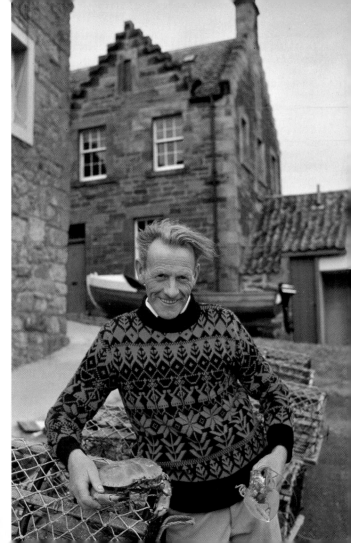

to say—crowns Great Britain. Its 30,000 square miles (about the size of South Carolina) contain 5.2 million Scots, one-tenth of the total United Kingdom population. Mountain barriers no longer fragment the country as they did in the heyday of the Highland clans, but formidable peaks certainly dominate the landscape. Ben Nevis, at 4,406 feet, is the highest mountain in Britain.

The wildly irregular coastline, forever pounded by the Atlantic and the North Sea, has both fierce cliffs and sweeping sandy beaches. The sea flows in to fill many of the country's 300 lochs (never called lakes locally). Along the west coast, visitors are surprised to find flourishing subtropical gardens—a bonus of the Gulf Stream close offshore.

Included in Scotland's territorial area are 790 islands, most of them visited only by sea birds; but 130 are inhabited, and a few are popular tourist

destinations easily reached by ferry or airplane.

Constitutionally entwined with England for nearly three centuries, Scotland in certain respects is still a land proudly unto itself. It prints its own currency and postage stamps (British versions, of course, circulate as well), maintains independent educational and judicial systems and its own church, and quite often speaks in ways even the English need dictionaries to decipher.

Since 1975, Scotland has been divided into 9 regions and 3 island areas. Within the regions are 53 districts, a confusing administrative reordering which dissolved such long-familiar counties as Perthshire and Aberdeenshire. To sort out any muddle, efficient tourist

Beautiful wind-lashed Duncansby Head is too remote for human flocks.

information centres operate all over the country.

Everywhere you'll encounter Scots who are enormously friendly and helpful to strangers. Smiles are genuine, humour is jovially sharp, and there always seems to be time to chat about where you're from and what you're up to.

Even in tiny villages you may be struck by how articulate the people are. This could well reflect the great value placed on education. (In the 17th century, they like to remind you, poor little Scotland had four universities while England still had only two.) And it's a rare Scot who doesn't have an inde-

pendent opinion on just about every issue.

Don't count on disproving the old cliché about the Scots being tight-fisted—or thrifty (depending on your point of view). On the other hand, personal generosity is something you'll experience almost everywhere. The coin of the realm is greatly respected in Scotland, and if you're hunting for bargains you'll be disappointed. That's true even about the golden "water of life" you buy right at the whisky distilleries.

Despite tax-inflated prices, the Scots do their best to live up to their hard-drinking reputations. Alcoholism is an acknowledged problem. Among other things, it contributes to a high divorce rate (about one out of every three marriages). Gambling is another local passion. Scotland's national Presbyterian church, the Kirk, spearheaded by stern traditionalists in the western Highlands and islands, campaigns ceaselessly against such social woes.

And, if there's anything which might qualify as a national mania, it's soccer. The merits of Glasgow's Celtic and Rangers inspire as much heated debate as politics, another inescapable public preoccupation.

Over the centuries, the Scots have touched on all corners of the globe: they were frontiersmen in North America, explorers in deepest Africa, pioneers in Australia. For various reasons, mostly economic, they've often settled far afield. Today about ten times as many people of Scottish birth or descent live abroad as at home. Scotland's contribution to world science, medicine and industry has been astonishing.

Above all what binds Scots together (though for centuries they spilled each other's blood) is love of their country. Many are unabashedly sentimental, despite the "dour Scot" image. The works of Robert Burns and Sir Walter Scott are perennial best-sellers. Current writers are constantly finding wondrous new aspects of that glen or this ben. Bonnie Prince Charlie and Mary Queen of Scots are endlessly ballyhooed.

Convinced that their homeland isn't far from paradise (perhaps excepting a wee bit of rain), Scots traditionally urge the departing visitor, "Haste ye back". After sampling the extraordinary beauty and diversity of Scotland, you'll want to.

Even in Scotland's northern areas the profusion of blooms is remarkable, as at splendid Cawdor Castle.

A Brief History

It all began in Scotland more than 8,000 years ago, and it has never been easy. The earliest settlers, drifting north from England or across from present-day Ulster, fished and hunted along the west coast.

By about 4000 B.C. more sophisticated immigrants from western Europe, Britain and Ireland had begun farming and raising stock in Scotland, using pottery and burying their dead in stone tombs. Recently, west of Aberdeen, archaeologists discovered remains of a huge timbered building from this era, 1,000 years before Stonehenge. Called Balbridie Hall, it is the oldest wooden structure ever found in the British Isles.

Scotland's famed megalithic monuments—Standing Stones of Callanish on Lewis in the Outer Hebrides and the Ring of Brodgar and Standing Stones of Stenness on Mainland in the Orkneys—were erected between 2000 and 1500 B.C. by a race which had evidently originated in the Mediterranean.

During the Bronze and Iron ages Scotland was settled by various tribes speaking forms of Celtic (which survives in Britain today as Gaelic and Welsh). Inhabitants south of the Forth-Clyde isthmus were Britons, those to the north became known as Picts. These primitive tribes weren't much of a match for the Roman legions who marauded north under Agricola and defeated the Picts in A.D. 84 at the battle of Mons Graupius in north-east Scotland.

As outposts against the troublesome Picts, the Romans built a line of forts across Scotland from Meigle (north-west of Dundee) to the River Clyde south of Loch Lomond. It was the northernmost point of their vast empire. They later withdrew to the line marked by Hadrian's Wall close to the present Scottish-English border.

Late in the 2nd century masses of Pictish warriors raided south across both lines, prompting a retaliatory assault under Septimus Severus in 208, the last major Roman incursion into Scotland.

The Scots entered the scene in the 5th–6th century. A Gaelic-speaking tribe from Ireland,

Ruins and standing stones at Clava Cairns indicate a busy prehistory.

12

they founded a shaky kingdom in Argyll called Dalriada that was constantly menaced by the Picts. But in 563 St Columba arrived from Ireland to bolster his fellow Celtic Christians. For over 30 years, from the remote western island of Iona, he spread the faith which would eventually provide the basis for the unification of Scotland. With its abbey and royal graveyard, tiny Iona remains one of the most venerated sites in Christendom (see p. 80).

The Norse Invasion

Scotland was among the areas repeatedly savaged from the late 8th century as Vikings swarmed over Europe. Permanent Norse strongholds were established in the Orkneys, Hebrides and northern mainland. The Scandinavian warriors greatly weakened the Picts in 839, enabling a Gaelic chief called Kenneth MacAlpin to become king of both the Scots and the Picts.

In 1018 at the battle of Carham, this unified kingdom under Malcolm II defeated the Northumbrians from the south and extended its domain to the present southern boundary of Scotland. Malcolm II's grandson Duncan II succeeded to the throne of Scotland. His murder by Macbeth inspired

the great Shakespearean tragedy.

Malcolm III, known as Malcolm Canmore, changed the course of Scottish history by marrying an English princess. This was the determinedly pious Queen Margaret, who later became a saint (see pp. 25–26). She and her sons brought powerful English influence and atmosphere to both the Celtic church and the monarchy as Scotland developed into a feudal kingdom.

Margaret's son David I (1124–53) is remembered for founding such great abbeys as Melrose and Jedburgh in the Borders (see pp. 36–37). King

David also encouraged the start of peaceful Norman penetration into Scotland. This did not mean a "Norman Conquest" as in England but the spread of French, the building of many castles and churches and eventually the absorption of still another culture into the Scottish mainstream.

The Shaping of Scotland

Progress, prosperity and the stirrings of a national consciousness marked the long reign of King Alexander III (1249–86). At the battle of Largs in 1263, Alexander's forces trounced King Haakon of Norway, forcing the Norsemen finally to abandon all the western islands. Under a peace treaty the Norse retained only the Orkneys and Shetlands which were acquired by Scotland some 200 years later.

Alexander's death in a riding accident touched off a succession crisis and a long and bloody struggle for Scottish independence. In the midst of the civil strife provoked by 13 rival claimants to the throne, King Edward I of England was invited to arbitrate. Taking advantage of the situation, he chose John Balliol to be his vassal king of Scots. But in 1295 Balliol made an alliance with France (then at war with England) and renounced his fealty to Edward. In retaliation, the English king sacked the burgh of Berwick, crushed the Scots at Dunbar, swept north seizing the great castles and carried off from Scone Palace

Battered but grand, Melrose Abbey survived bitter English assaults. **15**

the Sacred Stone of Destiny on which all Scots monarchs had been crowned (it's still in Westminster Abbey in London).

Chafing under military occupation, the Scots led by William Wallace revolted again in 1297, defeating the English at Stirling Bridge. But Edward routed Wallace at Falkirk the next year, English bowmen killing some 15,000 Scots. (In 1305, the outlawed Wallace was captured, taken to London and brutally executed; Edward had parts of his body displayed around Scotland.)

Then came Robert Bruce, another revered Scots champion—even though he sacrilegiously killed his rival in a church before having himself crowned king at Scone Palace in 1306. Forced to flee to Ireland, Bruce returned the next year to subdue his Scottish opponents. Edward died before he could deal with this new upstart, and his weak son, Edward II, was thoroughly defeated by Bruce's forces at the watershed battle of Bannockburn in 1314. With many personal heroics, Bruce kept hammering at the English until 1328 when Edward III signed a treaty recognizing Scottish independence. Robert Bruce died the following year, honoured as medieval Scotland's saviour.

The Stewarts

It was not a healthy time for Scottish kings. The Stewart kings, James I, II and III, who reigned successively between 1406 and 1488, all came to power while children and all died violently. James I was kidnapped and held in captivity for 18 years; after a brief reign he was murdered. James II was killed by an exploding gun; and James III was assassinated before he was 40.

During this period, Scotland extended its territorial boundaries to today's limits by taking the Orkney and Shetland islands from Norway in 1472. Many place names today recall the centuries of Norse occupation.

James IV (1488–1513) greatly strengthened and popularized the monarchy. In the western Highlands and islands, he succeeded in putting down the rebellious Macdonald clan chiefs, who had been calling themselves the Lords of the Isles since the mid-14th century. Against the English he didn't do nearly so well: in 1513, to honour the "auld alliance" with France, James led his Scottish troops in an invasion that penetrated only a few miles over the border to Flodden. The ensuing battle there, bitterly remembered, saw the

English under the Earl of Surrey crush the Scots. About 10,000 were killed including the king himself and most of the peerage. Flodden was the worst military disaster Scotland ever suffered.

That brought the infant James V to the throne. When he grew up he waged bloody struggles against the Scottish clans, had his own sister burnt for witchcraft, resisted Henry VIII's mushrooming Reformation, promoted local Scottish justice and married first one French woman, then a second called Mary of Guise. James died prematurely in 1542, six days after his wife had given birth to a daughter, his only heir.

Mary Queen of Scots
The adventurous life, loves and death of this queen, called Mary, have captivated generations of Scots. Henry VIII quickly tried to force a treaty betrothing her to his son. Infuriated when this failed, he sent his troops on violent rampages through southern Scotland. At the age of five, Mary was bundled off to France for safekeeping; in time, her pro-Catholic mother, supported by French forces, took over as regent. This increasingly angered many Scots.

As a teenager, Mary was married to the boy-heir to the French throne. But he died soon after becoming king, and in 1561 Mary, a devout young Catholic widow, returned to Scotland to assume her own throne. She found Protestant Reformation in full cry, led by the fiery John Knox. Roman Catholicism had just been abolished as the religion of Scotland and the French troops sent home.

Mary spent most of her seven years as resident Queen of Scots in Edinburgh's Holyroodhouse Palace. She insisted on practising her Catholic faith, but had no objections to religious freedom in her realm. In 1565 Mary married a controversial young nobleman, Henry, Lord Darnley. The next year she had a son, the future James VI. Darnley was involved in the murder of Mary's confidential secretary at Holyrood (see p. 31) and was himself killed in 1567. Many suspected Mary of conniving in the murder of her husband and doubts hardened when, a few months later, she married one of the ringleaders of the plot, the newly divorced Protestant Earl of Bothwell.

That was too much. Disgraced in Scottish eyes and condemned by the Pope, Mary **17** tried to flee from her subjects, some of them demanding her death by burning. She was captured, imprisoned in an island castle on Loch Leven and forced to abdicate in July 1567 in favour of her infant son. Seeking refuge in England where, at least to Catholics, she seemed to have a legitimate claim to the throne held by her cousin Elizabeth, Mary instead was kept in captivity for nearly 20 years and finally beheaded in 1587.

Toward Union with England

In the wake of Mary's departure, Protestantism became Scotland's official religion. After a period of rule by regents (1567–78), James VI became the first Protestant king of Scotland. When Elizabeth died in 1603, James as the heir rode south to claim the English throne as James I. He ruled his native land mostly at a distance, as did his successors of the Stuart (spelling changed under Mary Queen of Scots) family. But the Union of Crowns meant no instant harmony between the two traditionally antagonistic neighbours.

The turbulent 17th century in Scotland saw fierce church and political struggles. James's son Charles I (1625–49) pro-

voked the opposition of Scottish churchmen—and even rioting—with his attempts to impose an English prayer book. In 1638 the National Covenant signed by Scots around the country insisted on the right to their own form of Presbyterian worship. In England's civil war, the Covenanters at first backed Parliament against Charles, who was beheaded in 1649. The following year the Scots sided with Charles II, leading Cromwell to invade and crush their army at Dunbar. Scotland endured nine years of military dictatorship under Cromwell's Commonwealth.

Long after restoration of the monarchy in 1660, Scotland's bloody internal religious fighting continued. Extreme Covenanters in the Highlands were severely persecuted during the so-called "killing time". But when James VII/II was dethroned in the revolution of 1688, Presbyterianism was formally established as Scotland's state religion.

Highland clans were forced to take the oath of loyalty to the new king, William of

More than two centuries later, the evocative memorials of Scotland's final battle raise clansmen's tears.

Orange (1689–1702). When the small Macdonald clan of Glen Coe was slow to give its pledge, soldiers under a Campbell of Glenlyon slaughtered 38 Macdonalds including women and children. This Massacre of Glen Coe on February 13, 1692, among the blacker episodes in Scottish history, immeasurably deepened clan hatreds and Highland resentment of the monarchy.

In 1707, despite widespread Scottish opposition, England and Scotland signed the Act of Union which made them one kingdom, Great Britain, with the same parliament and flag. Dissolving their own parliament, the Scots would be represented as a minority in the two houses at Westminster according to a population and wealth ratio. But they kept their own courts and considerably different laws, and their national Presbyterian church was guaranteed. Today the union of the two countries sharing the same island seems to have been historically inevitable. But Scottish nationalism was not easily subdued.

The Risings

Four times in the next 40 years, the Jacobites (Stuart loyalists) tried to restore the exiled royal family to the throne, which was

now held by the originally German Hanoverian family. In 1708 the son of James VII, known as the "Old Pretender", arrived with a French invasion force in the Firth of Forth but was prevented from landing.

In 1715 the Jacobites had slightly more success under the Earl of Mar who, with some 12,000 men, managed briefly to hold Perth, Inverness and the north-eastern coast. They hoped for French help which never came. The Pretender arrived months too late to rally any more support among an apathetic or pro-government public, and after the inconclusive battle of Sheriffmuir (near Dunblane), the rebellion remembered as the "Fifteen" dissolved. A minor Highland rising in 1719 had the support of a small Spanish fleet but quickly failed.

The most serious Jacobite effort was the Rising of 1745 which became the stuff of heroic—and tragic—Scottish legend. It was led by the Young Pretender, Prince Charles Edward Stuart. Nicknamed ever since Bonnie Prince Charlie, this grandson of James VII was 24 years old when he sailed from France disguised as a divinity student to land in Scotland for the first time in July 1745. Determined to restore the house of Stuart, the prince started with nothing more than persuasive charm. Within two months he had rallied enough clan warriors to sweep through Scotland, occupying Perth and Edinburgh and defeating a government army at Prestonpans. In early November he invaded England. Quickly seizing Carlisle, Charles and his Highlanders drove all the way to Derby, 130 miles north of London, by December 4.

But Charles was over-extended and far outnumbered by English troops. Reluctantly he agreed with his brilliant tactician, Lord George Murray, to retreat north and by December 20 they were back in Scotland. Despite an impressive victory over the English at Falkirk in January, it was downhill now for Charles and the Jacobite cause.

At the battle of Culloden Moor near Inverness on April 16, 1746, the weary Highlanders were devastatingly beaten by superior government forces under the Duke of Cumberland. In less than an hour about 1,200 of Charles' men were killed; many others wounded and captured suf-

His philandering forgiven, Robert Burns is boundlessly beloved poet.

fered brutalities which earned Cumberland the lasting sobriquet "Butcher". The Forty-five was over, but strong memories linger.

Charles escaped, spending five months as a fugitive in the Highlands and western islands before sailing away forever aboard a French ship.

The Aftermath

Although Jacobitism was finished, Highlanders had to pay harsh consequences for joining the rebellion. The government disarmed and garrisoned the region, disabled the clan structure, suppressed Gaelic and even banned wearing of the kilt for several decades. From about 1780 for nearly a century, thousands of crofter (small farmers) families were forced to abandon their homes to make room for wealthier sheep farmers from the south, in what became infamous as the Highland Clearances. Some were evicted, many others emigrated in poverty to Canada, the United States and Australia. When Britain went to war with Napoleonic France, nearly 40,000 men were raised for new Highland regiments, fighting with great distinction.

In less troubled southern Scotland, Edinburgh began developing into a major cultural centre, which it remains to this day. Scottish scientists, literary figures, explorers and industrialists gained international renown. Individual Scots went south and contributed greatly to the life of the United Kingdom into which they had been absorbed.

A symbolic turning point **21**

came in 1822 when George IV made the first state visit to Scotland in well over a century. Tartans and clan regalia were paraded at Holyrood Palace

The impact of Scotland's oil boom can be seen at Peterhead; but most rigs are far out in the North Sea.

and even the king put on a kilt in festivities organized by Sir Walter Scott. Later Queen Victoria and Prince Albert "discovered" Scotland and bought Balmoral Castle which is still regularly used as a summer home by the royal family.

In recent decades Scottish nationalistic spirit has revived

again, and new dreams (as well as environmentalists' nightmares), have been inspired by the discovery in 1970 of major oil deposits beneath Scotland's sector of the North Sea. Tourism, always heavy from England, is now rapidly increasing from other countries. This has prompted a blossoming campaign to preserve and exhibit what remains of Scotland's intriguing historical heritage.

Scot, Scottish, Scotch?

As if they didn't have enough kings, lochs, bens and glens to confuse a visitor, they're rather insistent about what they call anything to do with themselves.

Harking back to that ancient Gaelic tribe (from Ireland), a *Scot* is a native of Scotland. So is a *Scotsman* or a *Scotswoman*.

Almost everything which comes from or is typical of Scotland is *Scottish*, as in Scottish hospitality, Scottish romanticism, Scottish thrift.

But when it comes to whisky, it's always *Scotch* whisky (but a *wee dram* will get the message across in any Scottish pub). Also permissible: Scotch egg, Scotch terrier, Scotch broth, Scotch tape.

It all seems perfectly straightforward—if you're a Scot with Scottish logic...

Where to Go

Scotland, 275 miles from north to south (not counting the islands) and as wide as 150 miles, is far too large and full of sights to "do" on a touring holiday unless it lasts for months. With or without a car, you're wise to concentrate on one or two areas. There's a very useful public transport system (see p. 122), air service connecting various mainland and island points, plus a variety of guided bus and boat excursions from most tourist centres.

Getting from place to place is often not nearly as speedy as maps might make it seem: many roads are just one-lane affairs with scooped-out "passing places" where you or the oncoming vehicle must pull over to let the other go by. Charming at first, this quickly becomes tiring if there's much traffic. More fun are the nonchalant sheep and cattle frequently wandering onto country roads.

This book describes sightseeing highlights in the areas of Scotland most visited by tourists. Local details are dispensed by an extensive network of tourist information offices.

Edinburgh

Elegant, civilized and even in spots "swinging," Scotland's proud capital surprises and pleases most visitors—particularly when the sun shines. Both the Old Town up against the mighty rock of Edinburgh Castle and the (not-very) New Town across the way are well worth exploring. You'll find some of the most impressive buildings in Europe and a markedly congenial atmosphere—an unexpected bonus in a city of nearly half a million people.

Edinburgh's seven hills look north over the great Firth of Forth estuary or south to gentle green countryside rising into hills. Everywhere you climb there's a fine panorama. From on high, you might well see one of the city's 24 golf courses—after all it *is* the most Scottish of games. Tour guides boast that Edinburgh is probably 1,500 years old and has been the capital of Scotland since 1437. They point out homes of famous people you never knew came from here. Despite all these echoes of the past, the city today seems decidedly young and vibrant. And it's at its liveliest—and most crowded—during the three-week Edinburgh Festival each August–September (see p. 93).

Many of the city's principal sights are within easy walking distance of each other; almost all can be reached by public bus. Throughout the day, excursion coaches depart from Waverley Bridge, near the local tourist information office.

Edinburgh Castle

Heavy with history, Scotland's most popular tourist attraction stands on an extinct volcano, high above the city. No one knows how long ago Edinburgh's history began on this great rock, but a stone fortification was definitely erected late in the 7th century and the first proper castle built in the 11th century.

Two Royal Scots guards, bayonets fixed on their unloaded rifles, are posted for your camera at the first gate leading up the cobblestoned rampways to the castle. The impressive black naval cannon poking through the ramparts have never been fired, but you'll see the cannon which booms out over the city every weekday to mark 1 p.m. Why isn't it fired at noon? "Remember where you are," quips the guide. "One cannon shot at one o'clock is much cheaper than 12 at noon."

Tiny **St Margaret's Chapel** 25

with its plain whitewashed interior is the oldest building in Edinburgh and the oldest church in use in Scotland. Built by the devout Queen Margaret in about 1076, it survived assaults over the centuries that destroyed the other structures on Castle Rock. The simply restored Norman chapel is kept decorated with flowers each week by Scotswomen named Margaret.

On the promontory here commanding one of Castle Rock's many grand views over Edinburgh stands **Mons Meg,** a stout cannon forged in the 15th century, probably in Flanders. The five-ton monster ingloriously blew up 200 years later while firing a salute to the Duke of York.

Close by is an oddity, the world's most spectacular canine graveyard. In a niche overlooking the city you'll find the Cemetery for Soldiers' Dogs with tombs of regimental mascots. Further along: the Lyon's Den where James VI kept his pet lion.

In the Palace Yard is the **Great Hall,** built in 1502, which claims the finest hammer-beam ceiling in Britain. The oak timbers are joined without a single nail, screw or bolt. Scotland's parliament met here for a century. Among the

arms on display is a hefty 900-year-old claymore (from the Gaelic word for broadsword), labelled only with "Do Not Touch". The adjacent military museum exhibits a vast array of regimental paraphernalia.

Queen Mary's Rooms in the royal apartments include a very small chamber where she

gave birth to James VI (later James I of England) in 1566. Not recommended if you feel cramped in a crowd.

The castle's greatest treasure, the crown, sceptre and sword of Scotland, are displayed in the **Crown Room.** At times more than 10,000 viewers a day file through here to see the oldest royal regalia in Europe. The gold and pearl crown has been altered since it was first used for the coronation of Robert Bruce in 1306. Charles II wore it for the last time in

Edinburgh's proud castle is the inescapable feature of city skyline.

1651. Popes Alexander VI and Julius II gave the sword and sceptre to James IV. In cases on the wall hang a huge necklace and other pieces of dazzling jewellery.

Note: Edinburgh Castle's entrance lies just beyond the **Esplanade,** formerly a site for the execution of witches, later a parade ground, now a modern parking lot where the celebrated Military Tattoo is performed during the annual Edinburgh Festival.

For a charge you can join a group being escorted by one of the witty and lore-loving palace guides, a great bargain. In summer, the castle opens at 11 a.m. on Sundays.

The Royal Mile

It's all downhill along the high ridge from Edinburgh Castle to the royal palace, Holyroodhouse. The Old Town's famous thoroughfare, its cobbles now smoothed, is actually about 1¼ miles long—the Scottish mile was longer than the English. Edinburghers of this area of high tenements and narrow closes (entryways) seem to take delight in recounting how the residents used to toss their slops and refuse from windows after a perfunctory shout of "Gardyloo!"—the local equivalent of *gare de l'eau.* That meant centuries of rampant disease and a decidedly unpleasant reputation for a city so graced with intellectual genius. Today, odourless, tidy and lined by historic buildings, the Royal Mile assumes five names as it descends: Castlehill, Lawnmarket, High Street, Canongate and Abbey Strand just before the palace.

On Castlehill the **Camera Obscura** atop the Outlook Tower offers a fascinating 25 minutes—in clear weather. After climbing the 98 steps to a darkened octagonal chamber, you'll enjoy living panoramas of Edinburgh projected onto a circular table-screen by a periscope-like device. The accompanying commentary is masterly.

Food and cloth merchants no longer hawk from stalls in the **Lawnmarket.** In James Court here (named after its builder, James Brownhill), Samuel Johnson once visited his biographer, James Boswell. Brodie's Close recalls one of Edinburgh's favourite stories. Deacon Brodie was a respected city official and carpenter by day, a burglar by night (having taken wax impressions of his clients' house keys). Finally arrested and

Careful restoration has preserved the charm of the Royal Mile.

condemned to death, Brodie thought he could escape death by wearing a steel collar concealed beneath his shirt. He was wrong. The city gallows, which he himself had designed, worked. Brodie's double life inspired R.L. Stevenson's *Dr. Jekyll and Mr. Hyde.*

It's a brief detour down George IV Bridge to the head-high statuette of **Greyfriars Bobby.** This Skye terrier waited by his master's grave in nearby Greyfriars Churchyard for 14 years until dying of old age in 1872. Admiring the dog's fidelity, authorities made Bobby a freeman of the city—meaning he had the vote long before women, they'll tell you.

Back along the Royal Mile, **St Giles,** the High Kirk of Scotland, dominates Parliament Square. Its famous tower spire was built in 1495 as a replica of the Scottish crown. The oldest elements of St Giles are the four huge 12th-century pillars supporting the spire, but there was probably a church on the site since 854. John Knox preached here and is thought to be buried in the rear graveyard. St Giles' soaring Norman interior with splendid stained glass is spectacular, filled with memorials recalling great moments of Scottish history. Most beautiful is the vaulted **Thistle Chapel,** ornately carved of Scottish oak. You'll see a stall for the queen and a princely seat for each of the 16 Knights of the Thistle, Scotland's oldest order of chivalry.

Farther down the Royal Mile are the popular Edinburgh Wax Museum, the Museum of Childhood with toys from yesteryear and Huntly House, the principal city museum.

The celebrated royal palace of **Holyroodhouse** began life about 1500 as a mere guest residence for the adjacent, now-ruined abbey. Much expanded and rebuilt in the 17th century, it has often housed visiting monarchs. During the summer, Holyroodhouse is closed to the public for the week or so that the Royal Family is in residence.

In the long Picture Gallery, snide comments abound as guides shepherd groups past 111 portraits purportedly of Scottish kings, dashed off between 1684 and 1686 by Jacob de Wet, a Dutchman who had imagination, brushes and paint.

Upstairs in King James'

Tower, connected by an inner stairway, are the apartments of Darnley and Mary Queen of Scots. A plaque marks the spot where the hapless Rizzio, Mary's secretary, was stabbed 56 times with a dagger. You'll hear all about it.

The New Town

Until late in the 18th century all of Edinburgh was confined to the crowded, unhealthy Old Town along the ridge from the Castle. The population, about 25,000 in 1700, had nearly tripled by 1767 when James Craig won a planning competition for an extension. With significant help from the noted Robert Adam, the resulting New Town has become the most complete complex of Georgian architecture.

Centre of it all is Edinburgh's main thoroughfare, ever-busy Princes Street. At the far end is Waverley Market Shopping Centre, a smart complex of shops and restaurants on two levels, with the railway station below.

A fetid stretch of water called Nor' Loch was drained and made into **Princes Street Gardens,** the city's attractive green centrepiece. Rising from

Within Holyrood's gates intrigue, romance and murder made history.

the gardens is the landmark spire of the **Scott Monument,** which has a statue of Sir Walter with his dog, statuettes of Scott's literary characters and 287 steps to the top. For climbing them you get a certificate and an excellent panorama. The celebrated **floral clock,** with some 24,000 plants, also adorns Princes Street Gardens.

A sloping road known as the Mound (formed from refuse during construction of the New Town) passes through the gardens. Here you will find the **National Gallery of Scotland,** a distinguished small collection of the great painters. Look for Van Dyck's *The Lomellini Family* with its five pouting members, Rubens' dramatically gory *The Feast of Herod,* Velásquez's striking *Old Woman Cooking Eggs* and four Rembrandt portraits. The English school is represented by Turner, Gainsborough and Reynolds, and you'll see numerous paintings by the city's own Henry Raeburn.

North of Princes Street spreads the neo-classical New Town. Its masterpiece is **Charlotte Square,** which enthusiasts proclaim "the noblest square in Europe". The 11 symmetrically façaded houses forming the square's north side are considered the finest accomplishment of Robert Adam, Scotland's esteemed 18th-century architect. **No. 7 Charlotte Square** has been converted by the National Trust for Scotland into an authentic Georgian show house. In the dining room you'll see an enviable table setting for eight of Wedgwood and Sheffield, and in the bedchamber a marvellous old medicine chest and an early 19th-century water closet called "the receiver".

The **Scottish National Gallery of Modern Art** occupies premises in Belford Road. The collection is ambitious, with an emphasis on Scottish and British work.

Along Inverleith Row extend the 75 acres of the much-admired **Royal Botanic Gardens** with perhaps the world's largest rhododendron collection, cavernous plant houses and a remarkable rock garden containing hundreds of meticulously cultivated specimens.

A colony of some 200 parading penguins is the main attraction at Edinburgh's famous **zoo,** set in rolling parkland in the western suburb of Corstorphine. Take your camera.

Shoppers and sightseers endlessly throng broad, stately Princes Street, heart and soul of the city.

The South-East

From Edinburgh there are many half-day or full-day bus excursions to points of interest in the countryside. One of the closest is to huge **Hopetoun House,** an outstanding Adam mansion near SOUTH QUEENS-FERRY (10 miles west of the capital). It contains fine origi-nal furnishings, paintings by Dutch and Italian masters and, on its 100 acres of grounds, four-horned St Kilda sheep and red deer.

Overlooking the loch at nearby **Linlithgow** stand the extensive ruins of the great fortified palace where Mary Queen of Scots was born in 1542. Alongside is **St Mi-**

Well-informed National Trust custodian likes to explain the "simple yet ingenious" 17th-century grinding gear at Preston Mill.

chael's, among Britain's best medieval churches, where an apparently well-documented ghost warned James IV not to fight England—shortly before he and so many Scots went off to be killed at Flodden.

Golf courses, sandy duned beaches and pleasant villages make **East Lothian** a popular holiday district. At pretty **Dirleton,** original stone cottages set off a large triangular village green beneath a ruined castle. In good weather, you can take a short boat excursion from NORTH BERWICK out around towering **Bass Rock** where some 8,000 gannets far outnumber the puffins, kittiwakes, shags and cormorants. Ashore within view, the formidable reddish ruins of 600-year-old **Tantallon Castle,** perched high on a seaside cliff. Queen Victoria visited this fortress of the Black Douglas clan in 1898, presumably peering as you will down into the well cut 90 feet through rock. Slightly to the east at the wild and beautiful **Seacliff Bay** you can walk along a rocky shore to what's said to be Britain's smallest harbour. In a pinch, it might hold four dinghies.

Inland the now-sleepy hamlet of **Whitekirk** still has its large church but no longer the reputed Holy Well which in the 15th century attracted tens of thousands of pilgrims, including Pope Pius II. Along a stream at East Linton you might inspect **Preston Mill,** restored as it was 350 years ago. It claims to be the oldest water mill in the country capable of producing meal. The busy town of **Haddington,** with its carefully preserved 18th-century atmosphere, offers a planned walk past a good number of its more than 100 buildings cited for their his- **35**

toric or architectural interest.

Green wooded farmland rolls on from Lothian into Scotland's southern Borders region, notably along the very scenic River Tweed, better known for giving its name to a twilled fabric. The hilly countryside around **Peebles,** a pleasant riverside resort, is worth exploring, particularly the beautiful Manor Valley. To the east along the Tweed near INNERLEITHEN stands **Traquair House,** which dates back some 1,000 years. Twenty-seven Scottish and English kings have stayed at Traquair, which is full of such intriguing things as a secret stairway from a priest's room and a 14th-century hand-printed bible.

Abbotsford, further down the Tweed past GALASHIELS, is the rather elaborate house where Sir Walter Scott spent the last 20 years of his life. Visitors may inspect his armouries and private rooms containing unusual items the author collected. Abbotsford is open daily except in winter.

The Border Abbeys

All founded in the 12th century during the reign of David I, Scotland's four great southern monasteries stand in varying degrees of ruin today. All are worth a visit. So obviously vul-

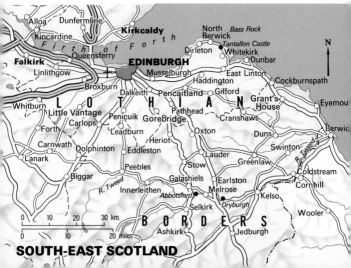

SOUTH-EAST SCOTLAND

nerable to invading English forces, the abbeys endured frequent sacking, were restored, then destroyed again.

At **Melrose Abbey,** strikingly set off by close-trimmed lawns, you can see part of the original high-arching stone church. There's a small museum crowded with relics and a lovely formal garden opposite the entrance.

Dryburgh, probably the most beautiful of the four abbeys, sits among stately beeches and cedars. Some of the monks' cloister survives, but little of the church. Here are the graves of Sir Walter Scott and World War I Field Marshal Earl Haig. At 593-foot Bemersyde Hill, reached from Dryburgh via GATTONSIDE by a beautiful tree-tunnelled road, you can enjoy spectacular **Scott's View,** the author's favourite riverside spot.

Only one arcaded transept tower and a façade remain in the market town of **Kelso** to suggest the dimensions of its abbey, the oldest and once the richest southern Scottish monastery.

Closer to the English border than the others on the Tweed, **Jedburgh Abbey** is a far more complete structure. The main church aisle, lined by a three-tiered series of nine arches,

Striking sandstone arches of abbey at Jedburgh, a convenient stop for motorists from north-east England.

is nearly intact. A neat old graveyard adjoins the abbey. Also in Jedburgh is Mary Queen of Scots' House, a two-storey stone museum containing a death mask made just after her execution in 1587 and her death warrant. Both the museum and Jedburgh Abbey are open year-round. **37**

Central Scotland

With its proud Renaissance castle commanding the major route between the Lowlands and Highlands, **Stirling** for centuries saw much of Scotland's worst warfare. The castle guides regale visitors with tales of sieges, intrigue and dastardly murders within the massive walls, and an audio-visual show just off the castle esplanade vividly portrays the savage saga. To take a break, you can walk the ramparts and gaze over the now-placid plains from this lofty fortress rock.

In contrast to sober Edinburgh Castle, Stirling's façade is festooned with all manner of weird, funny and nude if not rude carvings. Apparently James V, who built the palace, liked cherubs and demons. Most of the castle you tour today is "only" about 500 years old—though this towering rock was fortified at least four centuries earlier. It has changed hands more often than any castle in Scotland. James III was born here, his son and grandson, James IV and V, grew up here, Mary Queen of Scots was crowned here.

The Great Hall facing the upper square was once Scotland's grandest Gothic chamber, fit for sessions of parliament, but later it suffered through two centuries as a military barracks. It's now undergoing extensive restoration. In the banqueting section you'll see superb sterling silver pieces. Among the many displays in the fine military museum, watch for the old recruiting posters for the Argyll and

Sutherland Highlanders and for two ramshead snuff boxes.

Up until 1890, Stirling's **Auld Brig** built of local stone in the 15th century, was the only span across the River Forth. You can still walk over it.

Visible to the south of the castle is the battlefield of **Bannockburn.** Here the National Trust presents an audio-visual show that clearly explains the complex wars of independence culminating in Robert Bruce's epic victory over the English on this site in 1314. Commemorat-

Plan on spending at least an hour at "frivolous" Stirling Castle.

CENTRAL SCOTLAND

ing this proud Scottish triumph is a great greenish statue of Bruce in chain mail on horseback, along with the inscription of his declaration: "We fight not for glory nor for wealth nor for honour, but only and alone we fight for freedom, which no good man surrenders but with his life".

North of Stirling, 700-year-old **Dunblane Cathedral** is one of the finest Gothic churches in Scotland. It's about a century older than **Doune Castle,** a few minutes' drive to the east, a fortress-residence also excellently preserved. Its owner, the Earl of Moray, displays his first-class collection of vintage motor cars at a nearby museum.

Romantically popularized by Sir Walter Scott in "Lady of the Lake" and *Rob Roy*, the **Trossachs** is a region of lovely lochs and lochans, glens and bens. (It even includes Scotland's only "lake", the attractive Lake of Menteith, which was a perfectly ordinary loch until last century when for some reason they began calling it in the English fashion.)

The word "trossachs" probably means bristly places, after all its wooded crags. It's easy to get off the beaten track here, since beaten tracks are few. Try the road past Loch Arklet to INVERSNAID on Loch Lomond (a memorable dead-end route), reached via the wild ravine country between Loch Katrine and Loch Achray which is the core of the Trossachs. Salmon may be leaping up the easily accessible falls of Leny below Loch Lubnaig.

Loch Lomond, largest freshwater body in Great Britain, runs about 24 miles north to south. Most of its 30 isles and islets are privately owned. One has a good nature reserve. **Ben Lomond** (3,192 feet) looks companionably down on the sometimes choppy water, as do several lesser peaks. **Luss** is probably the prettiest of the little lochside villages. From BALLOCH, the busiest, you can join excursionists out to see the bonnie banks aboard the *Countess Fiona,* a motor steamer which makes the trip to Inversnaid and back two times a day in summer.

The tallest tree in Britain is alive, well and still growing at **Strone Garden** near CAIRNDOW on Loch Fyne. With all its foliage, you can't see the 188-foot top of this incredible grand fir *(abies grandis).* The giant has lots of lofty company in the garden's fine Pinetum.

Inveraray Castle, recovering from a very destructive fire in

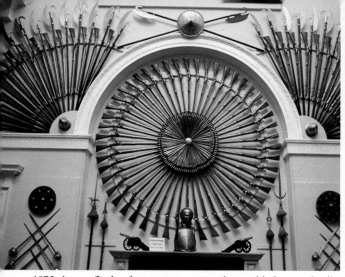

1975, has a flock of treasures to fascinate visitors. This home of the dukes of Argyll, just west of Loch Fyne, has been headquarters of clan Campbell ("uncrowned kings of the Highlands") since the early 15th century, although the present building dates only from 1790. The armoury, justifiably famous, contains an amazing array of broadswords, Highland rifles, shields, tassled medieval halberds and other exotic weaponry. The Turret Room's display of Wedgwood and other plate is stunning. The guides point out with pride the castle's best portrait, of the 6th Duke of Argyll. It's said he not only gambled away 4 million pounds but fathered 398 illegitimate children—which helps account for the 12 million Campbells around the world.

Farther south along Loch Fyne, delightful **Crarae Woodland Garden** has masses of azaleas, rhododendrons and roses. You can choose among three walks through the 40 hillside acres, always within earshot of a plunging brook.

At the great Bronze and Stone Age archaeological area near KILMARTIN, the best is hard to find: **Nether Largie North Cairn,** a ritual stone chamber used nearly 3,000

Inveraray's incredible armoury, 100 feet high, boasts 1,300 weapons.

years ago. Clambering down, you'll make out dozens of cup marks on the cover slab, along with carved axeheads which are thought to suggest Bronze Age magic. A human tooth was among the finds when this cairn was excavated. Ask directions for the track to the cairn through sheep pastureland; it's not far from the prehistoric sites of Nether Largie Cairn South and Templewood Stone Circle.

In this western area warmed by the Gulf Stream, exotic and sub-tropical plants flourish, nowhere more than at **Arduaine Gardens** on the coast below KILMELFORD. Highlights include rare rhododendrons, azaleas and prize magnolias.

Farther north well past the busy western isles' ferry port of OBAN, famous **Glen Coe** knifes inland from Loch Leven through impressive mountains. The scenery, complete with Highland sheep, red deer and golden eagles, attracts thousands of climbers and hikers. Geology, flora and fauna are **43** illustrated at a visitor centre operated by the National Trust, which owns thousands of acres of Glen Coe. In the steep valley, you'll find a memorial to the 1692 massacre of the Macdonalds. In bad weather, this is a bleak and even fearful place. A thatched-roof folk museum in the picturesque village of Glen Coe has clan Macdonald paraphernalia.

More often than not, clouds obscure the rounded and not very dramatic summit of **Ben Nevis,** at 4,406 feet the highest mountain in Great Britain. It's best seen from the north, but most easily climbed from the west starting near the bustling Highland touring centre of FORT WILLIAM. Caution is advised: bad weather closes in quickly atop Ben Nevis.

Inland, the long and thickly forested **Glen Garry** sheltering the Garry river and loch, is among Scotland's most wonderful mountain valleys. You'll agree with Robert Burns' en-

thusiasm about the **Falls of Bruar** cascading into the Garry near the lower end of the glen.

Blair Castle, just beyond, has put its little village of BLAIR ATHOLL on the map for countless excursion buses. Often reconstructed and restored, the white-turreted castle has long been the seat of the earls and dukes of Atholl. The present duke legally commands Britain's only "private army", an honorary and ceremonial Highland regiment of about 60

local riflemen and 20 pipers and drummers who march in their kilts very occasionally and haven't shot anybody for 170 years.

Your can tour 32 rooms in the castle, part of which dates back 700 years. It's jammed with Atholl family possessions amassed over the centuries: an extensive and exciting china collection, swords, rifles, antlers and stuffed animals, and portraits everywhere. Look for two rare colonial American powder horns, one with a fascinating map carved on it showing forts and settlements around Manhattan island, Albany and the Mohawk River.

A short drive south is the **Pass of Killiecrankie** where you'll want to walk wooded paths to the most spectacular parts of the gorge. A National Trust centre describes a noted Highlander victory here over the English in 1689.

Centrally located and proud of it, the crowded summer resort of **Pitlochry** is within reach of dozens of scenic and man-made attractions. In the town itself, you might visit the

It's thought Mary Queen of Scots also admired "Queen's View" in Perthshire, named after Victoria. **45**

Pitlochry Dam and Fish Pass, where each year about 8,000 salmon are electronically counted and watched through a windowed chamber as they leap up a ladder or through tubes towards their spawning grounds. The Pitlochry Festival Theatre is much admired for its spring-to-autumn performances.

To the west, a roadside promontory called the **Queen's View**—Victoria visited it in 1866—commands a glorious sweep down along Loch Tummel and over Highland hills. On a good day this is among the best panoramas in Scotland.

The delightful little village of **Fortingall** has history with mystery, Europe's "oldest living tree" and probably Scotland's finest thatched-roof cottages. The hamlet rests in Glen Lyon, the "longest, loveliest, loneliest" glen in Scotland by local account. Tranquillity reigns. You may want to stay for weeks. Persistent tradition, without scholarly confirmation, has it that Pontius Pilate was born in a nearby military encampment while his father was a Roman emissary to the Pictish king in the area. But there is no doubt about the authenticity of the very, very ancient yew tree surrounded by a rusty iron and stone enclosure in Fortingall's churchyard. Still growing now, though reduced in size, the yew certainly doesn't look its presumed age—3,000 years.

Don't miss **Dunkeld,** south of Pitlochry, with its splendidly restored "little houses", tan, grey and white, from the 17th century. They lead to a grand old cathedral which stands, partly ruined, amid tall trees, superior lawns and interesting gravestones alongside the River Tay. It's claimed that St. Columba preached in a monastery on this site. In Dunkeld's charming square is a useful information centre. Thomas Telford's arched stone bridge (1809) over the Tay here is much admired.

At the **Loch of the Lowes Wildlife Reserve** two wandering, wooded miles from Dunkeld, you'll have your best chance in Scotland to see an osprey. Binoculars are provided at a fine wooden hide where you can scan all kinds of water bird life and study trees where ospreys, migrating from Africa, nest.

After visiting Dunkeld—especially the cathedral's 9th-century choir —explore the forest trails nearby.

At the hamlet of MEIKLE-OUR, "one of the arboreal wonders of the world" lines the road: a gigantic beech hedge, at about 90 feet the highest anywhere, planted in 1746 and patently thriving.

Archaeology enthusiasts will appreciate the elaborately carved early Christian and Pictish stone monuments in the village museum at **Meigle.**

Just north of PERTH, acres of shiny green lawns surround the pale red sandstone of **Scone Palace,** as historic a site as any in Scotland. Here all, or nearly all, the kings of the Scots were crowned on the Stone of Destiny, which Edward I vengefully took away from Scone (pronounced Scoon) to London in 1296. (Some believe the stone now incorporated in the Coronation Chair in Westminster is not the original Stone of Destiny, which dated back to Kenneth MacAlpin in the 9th century, but a replica produced by the Scots at Scone for Edward to seize. These romantics suggest the real stone remains hidden in Scotland.)

Proceed past the temperamental peacocks to this ancestral home of the earls of Mansfield. The finest of the furniture is French; the marvellous china includes early Sèvres, Derby and Meissen. In

the decidedly Long Gallery, watch for more than 80 Vernis Martin objects which look absolutely like lacquered porcelain but in fact are *papier mâché*. This unique collection of vases and *objets d'art* won't ever be duplicated: the Martin brothers died in Paris in the 18th century without disclosing the secret of their varnish. Before leaving Scone, stroll through the grounds to the Pinetum, an imposing collection of California sequoias, cedars, Norway spruces, Japanese silver firs and other conifers in a gorgeous setting.

Out on the Fife coast, **St Andrews** is inevitably busy since it's known world-wide as the home of golf. Here the game of golf or something like it has been played for 500 years. Anyone can tee off on the Old Course at the Royal and Ancient Golf Club where so many epic championships have been held (see p. 85). This extremely pleasant seaside resort also has Scotland's oldest university (founded in 1411), and the great ruin of Scotland's largest-ever cathedral, built during the

12th and 13th centuries. James V and Mary of Guise were married here. The town's old castle features an escape-proof "bottle dungeon". In summer there's an arts festival, and the local theatre gets good reviews.

Picturesque fishing villages strung along Fife's south-eastern coast, called East Neuk, are favoured by holidaying families as well as golfers. **Crail,** where you're likeliest to find freshly caught lobster, is a friendly, quaint little port with a Dutch-style Tolbooth (courthouse-jail) tower and restored buildings which seduce photographers.

ANSTRUTHER (pronounced "Anster" if you're asking directions), once Scotland's herring capital, is very much worth a stop for its **Scottish Fisheries Museum.** You'll see a startlingly realistic fisherman's cottage of about 1900, magnificent ship models, whale tusks and a display explaining how trawlers trawl. From Anstruther you can take a motorboat excursion to the Isle of May, a bird sanctuary with 250-foot cliffs.

At PITTENWEEM, another venerable fishing harbour with impressive restoration, you often see masses of shrimp among the seafood brought in by the fleet to the thriving quayside market.

St Andrews has seen the élite of the golfing world; Anstruther's museum delights adults and kids.

49

The North-East

The "granite city" explains it-self when you see the building and houses of massive grey blocks everywhere in **Aberdeen.** Yet surprisingly, this solid metropolis farther north than Moscow is anything but som-bre: about a million roses plus other flowers like daffodils and crocuses flourish in such profu-sion that Aberdeen has won the coveted Britain-in-Bloom trophy six times.

Scotland's third city (pop. 210,000) is Great Britain's third largest fishing port, and that means the best show in town. Don't fail to make an early

morning visit (best about 7.30) to the huge harbourside **fish market.** Containers of fish by the thousand are unloaded from the weathered trawlers. You'll see huge triangular halibut, long black-grey "coaleys" (coalfish), gigantic skate, greyish-white ling, dogfish, turbot, whiting, cod, haddock and all

Aberdeen—tons and tons of fresh fish daily and grandiose grey granite.

the other edible denizens of the North Sea being iced, hauled, counted, bought and carried off by hard and hearty Aberdonians.

But even though it's thriving, the traditional fishing industry isn't why Aberdeen today is Scotland's boom city. Most of the 40,000 annual boat arrivals are involved in servicing the great oil rigs out to sea beyond the horizon. Ashore, the city's facilities have swelled to accommodate the influx of North Sea oil people, creating a rather odd international atmosphere for the thousands of tourists who arrive in the summer.

Touring Aberdeen on your own or by guided excursion, you'll inevitably see **Marischal College,** one of the largest granite buildings in the world. It's right in the heart of town. Built of a lighter-coloured variety known as "white granite" it forms part of Aberdeen University.

The other part is **King's College,** a much less granitic campus a short drive away in mostly medieval Old Aberdeen. Dominating the pleasant quadrangle is the beloved local landmark, the Crown Tower of King's Chapel. Knocked down in a storm in 1633, the structure was put back up with Renaissance additions. Within the chapel, look for the arched oak ceiling and the carved screen and stalls, outstanding medieval woodwork.

Nearby you walk through a very crowded graveyard to Aberdeen's cathedral, **St Machar.** First erected in 1357 but rebuilt mostly in granite the following century, it's described by scholarly guides as the "most marvellous fortified cathedral in western Europe". Capping the marvellous stone interior with its stained-glass windows is another oak ceiling described as heraldic, that is, bearing seals of kings and religious leaders.

Aside from the cathedral, nothing of importance was built of granite until about 200 years ago. Today half of Aberdeen's granite buildings came from **Rubislaw Quarry,** which opened in 1741 and finally ran out of stone in 1970. What remains is a mammoth hole, which you'll find surprisingly close to the centre of Aberdeen out along Queens Road. Now fenced off, unidentified and a bit overgrown, Rubislaw is awesome.

Aberdeen's 17th-century **Mercat Cross,** unusually ringed by a parapet engraved with the names of Scottish monarchs from James I to

James VII, is claimed to be the finest surviving burgh (chartered town) cross in Scotland. And Aberdeen has been a burgh for a long time: it received a charter from William the Lion in 1179.

You'll find Aberdeen's excellent tourist information centre at St Nicholas House on Broad Street.

The long, picturesque valley of the **River Dee** extending inland from Aberdeen to the high Cairngorm Mountains has been called Royal Deeside since Queen Victoria wrote glowingly about the area. She often holidayed at **Balmoral Castle** after Prince Albert, her consort, bought the huge estate in 1852 and refashioned the turreted mansion by the rushing river according to his own taste. The granite is local, lighter than Aberdeen's. From May 1 to July 31, if the royal family is not using Balmoral, the grounds are open to the public. Over the road, the modest granite **Crathie Church** attended by the royal family is unspoiled even though it's an inevitable tourist attraction.

Farther along the Dee toward Aberdeen, **Crathes Castle** has some of Scotland's most dramatic gardens, with giant yew hedges clipped just once a year by obviously skilled gar-

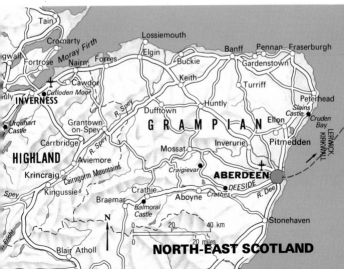

NORTH-EAST SCOTLAND

Often without publicity, members of Britain's royal family escape to Balmoral from London, knowing local folk will respect their privacy.

deners. The views from within the 16th-century tower house over these remarkable hedges are in themselves worth the visit. But look for the three famous rooms with painted ceilings, the carved oak ceiling in the top floor gallery and the 14th-century ivory Horn of Leys over the drawing-room fireplace.

To the north-west, near MUIR OF FOWLES, is the **Craigievar Castle.** Almost nothing has changed about this much-photographed seven-storey tower house since it was built in 1626. It doesn't even have electricity. Admired as a masterpiece of Scottish baronial architecture, the castle is panelled throughout in pine. An informative

guided tour is included in the entry fee to the castle. Unusual items you'll see: a metal head-and-neck device nicknamed "scold's bridle" used by Scottish husbands on their nagging wives, and three very rare "Craigievar tables", long, two-person gaming tables. Pink and slender, Craigievar is perhaps the loveliest of the 70 castles in north-east Scotland.

At PITMEDDEN north of Aberdeen, the rare 17th-century formal **garden** covers 3 sunken acres. Some 37,000 plants form elaborate floral designs patterned after those of Edinburgh's Holyroodhouse Palace, set off by close-clipped box hedges and shaven lawns.

On the often stormy coast south of PETERHEAD, you may have to ask directions to the **Bullers of Buchan** near Cruden Bay. These are plunging, wildly beautiful clefts in high, rugged sea cliffs. The screams of the marine birds echo up from the caverns. As a sign here warns, **55**

these cliffs are dangerous: footing can be slippery along the narrow pathways out to one of the most gorgeous and dramatic spots in Scotland.

Nearby, unmarked, down a bumpy if not muddy track from the village of CRUDEN BAY, stand the impressive reddish ruins of **Slains Castle** overlooking the coast. On a fine day, picnicking is inviting on grassy cliffs below the castle. But if the mist is blowing in from the sea swirling around the ruins, you'll appreciate the literary associations the castle has had with Dracula.

West of FRASERBURGH are two of Scotland's tiniest, most appealing fishing villages, **Pennan** and **Crovie.** A precipitous, narrow road hairpins down to Pennan's trim, white twin-chimneyed houses on a small bay. As at Crovie, there's not much to do aside from messing around with a handful of boats. Visitors are greeted with great friendliness by the fisherfolk who live on this little-known part of the coast. GARDENSTOWN, a bit to the west, is a pleasant, larger port.

Simplicity and tranquillity reign at Pennan where the fishing's fine and the seabirds outnumber people.

The Highlands

No longer really remote, Scotland's happily under-populated north offers superb scenery above all, but also the country's most amusing castle, most mysterious monster and most delightful distilleries. You reach almost everywhere through **Inverness,** capital of the Highlands since the days of the ancient Picts. Unless it's Sunday, stop for an hour in this busy centre to tour the small modern **Museum and Art Gallery** in Castle Wynd. In a fascinating exhibition of Scottish Highland history from the Stone Age, you'll brush up your clan lore and see dirks and sporrans, broadswords and powder horns.

Strategically sited where the River Ness joins the Moray Firth, Inverness is not shy about exploiting the submarine celebrity presumed to inhabit **Loch Ness** to the south. "Nessie" T-shirts and posters and all kinds of monster bric-a-brac are on sale. Excursion boats make regular monster-spotting cruises down the loch. Careful count is kept of Nessie sightings: in recent times, there have been more than a dozen a year considered reliable—and some very persuasive photographs.

With modern science in the form of sonar and sophisticated underwater cameras now apparently closing in on the mystery, most experts involved seem to agree that not one but a number of large aquatic creatures indeed roam the very murky depths of Loch Ness, surviving by eating eels and various fish. Eight rivers feed this fresh water loch, bringing in millions of peat particles which, while not polluting, reduce visibility to zero below 40 feet. Some 23 miles long and roughly a mile across, Loch Ness is generally about 700 feet deep—though in one area the silted bottom measures almost 1,000 feet. All that means enough space for large families of the monster which has intrigued people ever since it was first reported sighted in the 6th century—by no less revered a traveller than St Columba.

About 5 miles east of Inverness at now-tranquil **Culloden Moor,** Jacobite clan headstones, a mini-museum and an information centre recall the 1746 victory of Cumberland's redcoats over Bonnie Prince Charlie's Highlanders—the last major battle fought on United Kingdom soil. The young prince's adventures are retold in a stirring 15-minute film. Near the battlefield is the impressive **Clava Cairns** archaeological site. Three once-domed tombs are encircled by standing stones. It's fascinating and a bit eerie to stand in one of these silent burial chambers dating from between 1800 and 1500 B.C., and wonder.

"Three out of four Ghosts prefer **Cawdor Castle**" announces the sign at its authentic drawbridge entrance. And so should you. This is the only castle in Scotland that keeps you laughing as you learn. Don't fail to read the signs describing what you're seeing. They will keep you from brooding about the fact that in this fortress home of the earls of Cawdor, Shakespeare had Duncan murdered by Macbeth.

For your safety, you'll have to forego the tempting spiral steps up to the tower which has survived since 1454. The tower's Thorn Tree Room a stone vault enclosing a 600-year-old Hawthorn tree. The castle grounds have outstanding flower and kitchen gardens, a nature trail and even a pitch-and-put course. Your good mood will be enhanced at

58

You may not see Nessie at Urquhart Castle, but you won't miss the Don Quixote tapestries at Cawdor.

nearby **Cawdor village** where the stone cottages, cemetery and even cows are delightful.

For salmon and whisky, Scotland can offer you nothing better than the **River Spey.** Driving along this beautiful valley of ferns and old bridges you'll want to stop to watch anglers casting their long lines into this fastest-flowing river in the British Isles and, often enough, hauling in a shimmering salmon. Nestling among the trees on the hillsides are slate-roofed buildings with pagoda chimneys. Here they produce the finest of all the fine Scotch whiskies, or so local enthusiasts insist.

In this area, what's promoted as the world's only

After a tour of the Spey Valley, many visitors are ecstatic about the final product—but somewhat hazy about the mechanics of the distilling process.

whisky trail takes in four or more distilleries where you watch malt being distilled by a process basically unchanged for 500 years. Usually, you're invited to enjoy a free wee dram. Local tourist offices know which distilleries will accommodate visitors and when they're closed for maintenance (annual shutdowns last up to 6 weeks, often in July-August). If you're lucky, in the cooperage you'll see a cooper (cask maker) fashioning oak staves into a

cask: by law a spirit can't be called whisky and sold until it has been aged in oak for 3 years. According to the experts, the best maturity for Scotch is about 10 years. Around the malt centre of DUFFTOWN they still like to quote this old saying: "Rome was built on seven hills, Dufftown stands on seven stills"—although at recent count there were eight distilleries.

The popular **Landmark Visitor Centre** at CARRBRIDGE features a multi-screen film about Highland history, a nature trail and an exhibition of modern sculpture in a woodsy setting.

Aviemore is probably the most elaborate and modern holiday centre in Scotland, open all winter as well for skiing in nearby mountains. On a clear and not windy day, try a chair-lift ride up into the high Cairngorms where rangers conduct walks.

Seven miles south is the excellent **Highland Wildlife Park** at Kincraig with a drive-through area (don't leave your car, close the windows if animals approach). It may remind you of a game park in Kenya—except for the radically different wildlife. You should see all or most of these animals living wild or semi-wild: red deer, Highland cattle, ibex, soay **61**

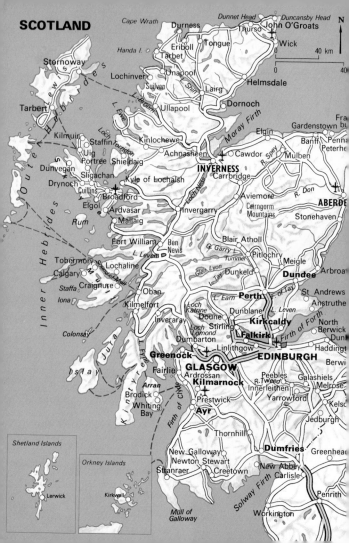

sheep, Przewalski's wild horses, European bison and mouflons (forebears of domestic sheep). Stars of the walk-through section include arctic foxes, bears and wildcats.

Moving west from Inverness to the coast, the dramatic **Loch Torridon** area is noteworthy for its red-brown sandstone and white quartzite mountains hundreds of millions of years old. If you stop by the charming and peaceful lochside hamlet of **Shieldaig,** opposite a National Trust nature reserve islet, you may be tempted to tarry.

The Gulf Stream works its warming magic again at **Inverewe Gardens,** a colourful subtropical oasis overlooking Loch Ewe on the same latitude as Juneau, Alaska. Late spring and early summer when blooms abound are best for a visit. Highlights include the gigantic magnolias and the exotic Himalayan Hound's Tooth.

At a fine wooded spot just a minute's walk off the highway below Loch Broom you'll find the **Falls of Measach,** plunging 200 feet into an awesome chasm called Corrieshalloch Gorge. It's worth a long look from the suspension bridge.

The Falls of Measach, one of Scotland's most dramatic sights.

Kilts and Tartans

For the Scotsman, Highland dress is not just an item of folklore to be brought out of mothballs on ceremonial occasions. It's everyday wear for some and the standard uniform of certain Scottish regiments. You'll probably see at least one pipe and drum band arrayed in kilted splendour.

Day-time Highland dress consists of a knee-length kilt, matching vest and tweed jacket, long knitted hose (with a knife stuck in the right stocking) and garters. The kilt is held up by a belt, and a sporran (purse) hangs from the waist. Sometimes a plaid, a sort of tartan rug, is flung over the shoulder.

Authentic tartans are registered designs. Each clan—originally a loose organization based on a family—had its own pattern. As the years went by and the clans subdivided, many variations (setts) of the tartans were produced. Today, it's estimated that there are more than a thousand setts.

While a certain amount of commercial gimmickry surrounds the tartan business, you may in fact have a genuine clan association—even if your family name seems far removed from Campbell, Macdonald or Stewart.

Scotland's most memorable scenery is probably along the jagged **north-west coast** above ULLAPOOL, a little fishing port doubling as ferry terminal for the Outer Hebrides. Whenever you can, take the secondary roads closest to the shore. You'll wind through extraordinarily beautiful country filled with mossy rocks, ferns and hundreds of tiny lochans. The first section goes through the Inverpolly Nature Reserve. Strange stories are told about gorgeous **Suilven,** the mount looming over the wild landscape near LOCHINVER (why don't animals graze on its slopes?). From tiny TARBET you may find an excursion boat going out to **Handa Island,** a teeming bird sanctuary with huge sandstone cliffs and sandy beaches.

You can reach mainland Scotland's north-western extremity, **Cape Wrath,** by ferry and minibus in the summer. Go on a clear day—from the great cliffs here, the birdwatching and the seascape are superb. This area contains some of the world's oldest rocks.

Near the friendly hamlet of DURNESS, **Smoo Cave** has a beautiful setting at the end of a

The romantic ruins of Varrich Castle near Tongue.

dramatic sea inlet. The "gloop-hole" through the cathedral-like limestone roof of the large outer cavern gets its name from the noise of air rushing up through it at high tide. Without venturing into the second cave, you can photograph its 80-foot waterfall from the entrance.

At the end of World War II, some German submarines put into deep and scenic **Loch Eriboll** to surrender to the Royal Navy. Further east, the coastal scenery around the **Kyle of Tongue** is glorious.

A lighthouse with stout red foghorns stands on a windy promontory called **Dunnet Head,** the northernmost mainland point in Scotland. Sheep graze here overlooking a serious sea, birds by the dozen swoop past, and if there's no mist you'll see Orkney on the horizon.

Nearby **John O'Groats** is far better known, although it just isn't quite the northern end of Great Britain. The sign here, which seems to be altered occasionally, declares that it's 874 miles to Land's End, the greatest distance between any two points in Britain (overland). Around the John O'Groats post office-cum-grocery store you'll hear lifeboat sagas—many ships have sunk in gales off this coast.

Close by is **Duncansby Head,** the most north-easterly point, where you should be allowed into the clifftop lighthouse in the afternoon. Be warned that if the foghorn blows while you're here, you won't soon forget it. Offshore the unusual pillar-like Stacks of Duncansby make a good photograph.

Inland and much to the south, make a short detour from the angling centre of LAIRG to **Shin Falls** where, with luck, you'll see sizeable salmon leaping up low, churning falls along the lovely river.

The South-West

Glasgow

Scotland's largest urban centre (pop. 765,000) is a city transformed. The brick Victorian buildings, architecture of a golden age of fortunes made in shipbuilding, iron and steel, are being restored to their former glory. The River Clyde runs clear, and the air is now pollution-free.

The heart of Glasgow is pleasant **George Square** where you'll find a dozen statues of famous people. (An outsize Sir Walter Scott towers above them all.) Nearby you can catch a city bus tour. Guides describe some bizarre local murders, boast that the River Clyde purification scheme is going so well that salmon thrive downstream, and point out Glasgow Green, one of the city's 62 parks and the oldest in Great Britain.

Glasgow's fine Gothic **cathedral,** in part almost 800 years old, holds the tomb of St Mungo, the city's patron. More ornate are the mausoleums of Glasgow's Victorian worthies, in the Necropolis behind the cathedral.

Among many Victorian buildings, Charles Rennie Mackintosh's **School of Art** is highly acclaimed.

One of Glasgow's major sights is also among the newest: the **Burrell Collection** in Pollok Park, a spectacular art museum opened in 1983. An innovative building was specially commissioned to hold the thousands of pieces amassed earlier this century by Scottish shipping tycoon Sir William Burrell. He bought

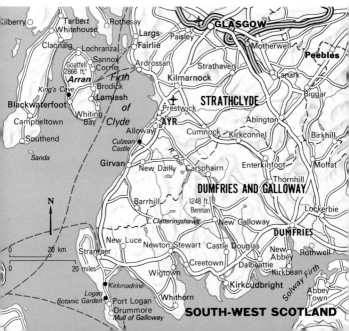

SOUTH-WEST SCOTLAND

up everything from Greek statues to Impressionist paintings—often at bargain prices.

Also worth a visit is the **Art Gallery and Museum** in Kelvingrove Park—one of Europe's outstanding collections of painting. The Rembrandts include his dark, powerful *A Man In Armour,* the alarming *Carcass of an Ox* and a rather prim *Self Portrait.* Van Gogh's *Portrait of Alexander Reid* is here: so are seven Degas works including *The Rehearsal* and *The Green Ballet Skirt* in a dazzling 19th-century French display: Frans Hals' dashing *Portrait of a Gentleman* among the Dutch;

Bellini and Giorgione works from the Venetian school; and Salvador Dali's striking *Crucifixion.*

At the Transport Museum, nearby, you can see the world's oldest bicycle.

Even several hours aren't enough at Glasgow's superb Art Gallery.

Arran

Surprisingly unspoilt, the isle of Arran close offshore in the Firth of Clyde offers a little bit of most of the loveliest things in Scotland. Regular car ferries travel to Arran's capital of BRODICK from ARDROSSAN on the Ayrshire coast in 55 minutes; in summer a smaller ferry links northern Arran to CLAONAIG in Argyll.

Green hills with a few scattered houses slope up behind Brodick's broad bay—in utter contrast to the Glasgow suburban sprawl you've just left behind. Arran's inhabitants number about 3,500, only slightly more than the number of red deer which roam wild in the island's beautiful mountain glens. Even in a car you can visit one of the best: **North Glen Sannox** between LOCHRANZA and SANNOX, where stags and hinds are often seen.

But this is pre-eminently an island for hill walkers or climbers. There are 10 summits over 2,000 feet and dozens of recommended ridge routes. Among the hundred or so bird species known to frequent Arran are peregrine falcons and a few rare golden eagles. Seals like the rocks around Arran's 50 miles of coastline, which you can circumnavigate by car. Basking sharks are seen off- **69** shore in summer. For archaeology fans the island has Neolithic chamber tombs and other ancient sites.

Standing above its bay amid grounds full of rhododendrons, azaleas and roses, **Brodick Castle** opens a handful of rooms to public viewing. But if you've seen other major Scottish castles, you might pass this one up and concentrate on the fine woodland and formal gardens.

Arran's most dramatic scenery is toward the north, topped by the highest mountain, **Goatfell** (2,866 feet). In the south the topography is gentler, with pleasant hills around the resort villages of LAMLASH and WHITING BAY.

Towards the island's southwest corner on a wild, cliff-backed coastal strip are the **King's Caves,** traditionally said to be where Robert Bruce watched a spider try and try again—which taught him how to deal with his and Scotland's destiny. Go there on a bright day. It's a bracing 20-minute walk from the place where you leave the car. The cathedral-like main cave of yellow, green and grey rock has a creaking iron gate to keep wandering sheep out. No human habitation is in sight, and nothing seems to disturb birds diving into the sea for fish.

Dumfries and Galloway

Back on the mainland, just south of the thriving coastal town of AYR you'll enter **Burns Country.** In this south-western area Robert Burns, beloved national poet, was born, lived most of his very full 37 years and died in 1796. Here are all the echoes of his narrative poem *Tam o' Shanter,* including the Auld Brig o' Doon which has spanned the River Doon in Alloway for some 700 years. You'll learn that Burns, perhaps excessively, liked his wee dram and bonny lassies, which nowadays seems to enhance his already monumental reputation in Scotland.

In **Alloway** you can visit Burns' carefully preserved birthplace, a whitewashed cottage with thatched roof, and a museum devoted to the poet. You'll see the little box bed where Burns and three of his brothers slept as small children, and such 18th-century implements as a butter churn and a turnip sowing machine. The original of "Auld Lang Syne" is among the mass of Burnsiana in the museum. Even his razor and shaving mirror are displayed.

Nearby at the new Land o' Burns Centre, with its accomplished audio-visual show about the poet and his work, you can decide how much more of the Burns' Heritage Trail to follow down to Dumfries where he died.

One of Scotland's foremost tourist attractions, **Culzean Cas**tle towers above the sea on a rugged stretch of the Ayrshire coast. With it are a Country Park of over 500 acres and stately formal gardens. Considered a Robert Adam master-

Within sight of Scotland's industrial belt, pastoral and unpolluted isle of Arran attracts family holidaymakers from all over Britain.

work, the castle dates mostly from the late 18th century and is now a National Trust property. The half-hour guided tour begins in the castle's armoury. You'll notice both Corinthian and Ionic columns on the famous oval staircase. The best room is the circular saloon with its windows overlooking waves of the Firth of Clyde breaking on the rocks 150 feet below.

Upstairs is an exhibition honouring Dwight D. Eisenhower for his role as Allied Supreme Commander in World War II. In the summer, on Sunday afternoons, a pipe band performs on the large sunken lawn of the Fountain Court just below the castle.

Unwisely overlooked by many tourists, south-western Scotland has beautiful shorelines, moor and forest scenery, and a castle with one of Rembrandt's great oils. It also claims milder weather than other areas. On the peninsula called the Rhinns of Galloway, the **Logan Botanic Garden** has Scotland's best collection of tree ferns and, among many palms and other warm-weather

species, glorious magnolia from western China. A nearby natural tidal pool called Logan Fish Pond features some amazingly tame fish that eat from a keeper's hand. At seaside PORT LOGAN (pop. 59) with its little yellow houses, three's a crowd at what's probably the smallest post office in the United King-

Grateful Scots gave Eisenhower an apartment in Culzean; when here he watched dancers like this lass.

dom. It measures about two yards square. From Scotland's most southerly point, the high-cliffed Mull of Galloway, you can see the Isle of Man—on a very clear day.

On a peaceful, pastoral hill midway up the peninsula there's a stone chapel containing the **Kirkmadrine Stones,** some of Scotland's oldest Christian relics: three inscribed stones and various fragments dating back to the 5th century.

South-east of NEWTON STEWART, the small Creetown Gem Rock Museum is unusual, if not eccentric. Apart from a celebrated rock assortment (including a chunk of the world's oldest, south-western Greenland felspar dating back 3.7 billion years), you'll find the world's largest collection of walking sticks: Gladstone's, Churchill's and Charlie Chaplin's are among those on display.

In the summer, motor cars (no buses or caravans) can take the scenic 10-mile **Raiders Road** forest drive from either CLATTERINGSHAWS DAM or BENNAN near MOSSDALE for a small charge.

It's worth making a detour to the north-west to see the pink sandstone **Drumlanrig Castle,** on an estate near THORNHILL with spacious lawns patrolled by sheep. Of all the treasures in this 17th-century mansion, you'll linger longest over Rembrandt's *Old Woman Reading* on the main stairway, with a fine Holbein nearby. In the drawing room, examine two black ebony inlaid cabinets which came to Scotland from Louis XIV. Napoleon's dispatch box is also here, a gift from Wellington to the castle owner.

South of Dumfries are the lovely red-sandstone ruins of **Sweetheart Abbey,** founded in the 13th century by the Lady of Galloway. It was dedicated to the memory of her husband, John Baliol, whose heart she carried around with her until she died.

On the other side of the River Nith along the coast, the **Ruthwell Cross,** named after its hamlet, is kept in a pretty little church surrounded by weathered tombstones. This great Dark Age monument, carved out of brownish-pink stone some 1,300 years ago, stands 18 feet high and is covered with sculpted figures and runic inscriptions. You may have to ask at a cottage along the lane for the key to the church.

On Skye, thatched roofs are mostly museum items but peat is still cut.

Inner Hebrides

⚲ Skye

This most-loved Highland island is outrageously beautiful—whenever *un*loved mists
are not swirling around its star-
tling hills and idyllic glens. Sto-
ried Skye is a 5-minute ferry
trip from KYLE OF LOCHALSH

or half an hour from MALLAIG.
Even if you can't stay, Skye is
worth a day trip.

Scenic honours go to two
remarkable ranges of peaks:
the Cuillins in the south, the
Quiraing in the north. They
make the island a hiker's or a
rock climber's idea of paradise.
Within the rugged **Cuillins** is

Loch Coruisk, reachable by a considerable overland trek or by boat from ELGOL. Some say this oblong stretch of blue-black fresh water is the prettiest lake in Britain. A few bushy islets decorate its surface. Isolated by high hills all around, Coruisk has a beauty which may seem rather eerie.

The **Quiraing** hills, more easily approached, dominate the landscape just north of the secondary road between STAFFIN and UIG, ferry port for the Outer Hebrides. You'll have a peaceful, out-of-the-world feeling walking among sheep on the grassy slopes of these dramatic hills.

In the far north at KILMUIR are the grave and monument of Skye's romantic heroine Flora Macdonald, who smuggled the fugitive Bonnie Prince Charlie to safety disguised as her female servant. Also in the north you're most likely to encounter traces of the Gaelic language and culture now being revived.

On the picturesque coast of Staffin, the **Kilt Rock** is a curiously fluted cliff with a waterfall plunging to the sea far below. Caution is wisdom on this lofty green ridge.

A mile further on, the Lealt Falls tumble down a long and accessible ravine into the sea at a pretty little cove. It's said salmon can sometimes be seen leaping here. Closer to PORTREE, Skye's capital, you'll see a giant grey-black rock pinnacle called **Old Man of Storr;**

Here on Mull, or anywhere else, the Scottish sheepdogs get the job done. **77**

there's a forest walk in the vicinity. Portree on its attractive inlet and BROADFORD are popular touring centres, but the island has many quieter places to overnight.

No castle in Scotland has been inhabited by the same family for as long as **Dunvegan Castle,** stronghold of the chiefs of MacLeod for more than seven centuries. On display within this sturdy lochside fortress is the Fairy Flag, a fragile remnant of silk believed to have been woven in Rhodes in the 7th century. It saved the MacLeods in clan battles twice, they say, and still has the power to do it one more time. More down-to-earth is the grim 16-foot-deep dungeon into which prisoners were lowered from an upstairs chamber.

From Dunvegan pier small boats make frequent half-hour trips to offshore rocks and islets where, if you're not noisy, you'll be able to get very close to seals. There are usually about 20 of them here, sometimes as many as 200. The seals also appear, less regularly, at spots all round Skye's 1,000 miles of indented coastline.

In the south, two off-track seaside hamlets called ORD and TARSKAVAIG are worth visiting on a clear day for their splendid views of the Cuillins.

Mull

Peaceful moorland glens among serious mountains, unusually appealing shorelines and one of Scotland's prettiest ports are among the attractions of this large western island. From Oban, the regular ferry takes 45 minutes to CRAIGNURE on Mull, and there's a 15-minute ferry link between FISHNISH POINT and LOCHALINE across the Sound of Mull. In summer boat excursions go to several popular smaller islands from Mull.

Tobermory (pop. 700), the charming little "capital", snuggles in a harbour ringed by forested hills and protected by flat, green Calve Island. Regattas are held here, film-makers have used the location, and golfers enjoy a superior seascape from links just above Tobermory. Somewhere deep beneath the mud at the bottom of the harbour, you'll inevitably hear, is an enormous treasure: in 1588 a gold-laden galleon from the Spanish Armada sank here, but salvage efforts ever since have failed.

Calgary, to the south-west, which has probably the best of Mull's sandy beaches, inspired the name of the Canadian city about a century ago.

If you're driving and aren't rushed, by all means take the

long coastal road bordering **Loch Na Keal.** It's slow but scenic going, along a single track beneath lonely cliffs and hills mauve with heather. Dozing sheep only reluctantly get up out of your way. If you happen to see an islander or two—called Muilleachs (pronounced Moolucks)—you might hear Gaelic, which is still spoken on Mull particularly by the older generation.

Quite close together at the eastern point, visible from the Oban ferry, stand Mull's two castles that are open to the public. **Duart,** the more imposing on its promontory, is the restored home of the chiefs of clan Maclean and dates back to the 13th century. **Torosay Castle,** in a sheltered garden, was built last century and often visited by not-yet-famous Winston Churchill.

Tobermory port—an artist's haven.

⚓ Iona

Precious to Scots and revered by Christians much farther afield, this tiny, serene island lies just off the south-western tip of Mull. From Ireland to Iona in 563 came St Columba and about a dozen followers, bringing the Christianity which would spread through Scotland (and also, quite probably, the Irish secret of distilling whisky). Some 60 Scottish, Norwegian, Irish and French kings are buried on this sacred isle. The last was Duncan, murdered in 1040 by Macbeth. Centuries of Viking and other onslaughts have left no trace of the earliest religious communities.

It takes seven minutes by sometimes bumpy passenger ferry (no cars) to reach Iona from Mull, or there are excursion boats from Oban. The major things to see: Iona's mostly 15th-century abbey, seemingly intact as restored but needing extensive first-aid; a small Norman chapel probably built in 1072 by Queen Margaret; attractive ruins of a 13th-century nunnery; St Martin's Cross carved in the 10th century, and Reilig Odhrain, the graveyard where royalty, Highland chiefs and more recent islanders are all buried.

Within the abbey is a pleasant little Benedictine cloister.

On a good day, stroll from here to North End where there are beaches of sparkling sand. Most of Iona's inhabitants (less than 100) live in the cluster of stone houses by the ferry landing. Sheep, cattle and a few fishing boats tell of occupations, although in summer most islanders are involved with the throngs of visitors. A few thousand pilgrims and religious students arrive to spend some time each year with the thriving abbey community.

Long owned by the ducal Argyll family, this 1,900-acre island has recently become the property of the government to preserve "for the nation". When Samuel Johnson visited Iona in 1773, he wrote: "That man is little to be envied whose patriotism would not gain force upon the plain of Marathon, or whose piety would not grow warmer among the ruins of Iona."

From Iona you can take a one-hour boat trip around nearby **Staffa** island, with its dramatic Fingal's Cave which inspired a celebrated Mendelssohn overture. You can also get to Staffa from Mull or Oban.

The sacred isle of Iona, burial ground of Scotland's early kings.

What to Do

Wherever you're staying in Scotland, particularly from spring to autumn, there's almost *too* much to do. Lists of the year's scheduled events of interest to visitors fill two thick Scottish Tourist Board booklets, and you'll come across many others local happenings as you travel around.

On summer weekends all around Scotland, competitions in tugging, sprinting, leaping and tossing draw large, enthusiastic crowds.

Special Events

Even if you only want to get away from it all on holiday, make at least one visit to a Highland Games, staged at various points around the country during the summer months. This can be Scotland at its most enjoyable. Aside from kilted titans tossing a huge pine trunk—the famous caber—and grunting through tugs-o'-war and other strenuous athletic endeavours, you'll see pipe and drum bands, Highland dancing even by small children, and more doughty old lairds and saucy

young lassies dressed in tartans than you'll have film to photograph. Members of the royal family often attend the Braemar Highland Gathering. Best of all are the agricultural shows and sheepdog trials which sometimes accompany Highland (or Lowland) gatherings.

Throughout the summer there are country fairs and common riding (when local folk ride the ''marches'' or boundaries of their town) in the Border region. In July, the Scottish Transport Extravaganza at Glamis Castle—exhibition of vintage vehicles, sale of vehicles, competitions, etc.—is the largest event of its kind in Scotland. Elsewhere there are special excursions to Scotland's historic houses and gardens, cruises on lochs and firths; flower shows; nature walks; geology, botany and bird-watching expeditions; tours on elderly steam trains; arts and crafts workshops; kilt-making demonstrations; whisky distillery tours, dozens of museums, reconstructed mills and crofter cottages. Edinburgh and Dunfermline have brass-rubbing centres. Prowling the foreshore you'll spot shells and odd marine life; inland with luck you might even find gems and semi-precious stones.

Sports

With nary a nod at a castle, museum or the Edinburgh Festival, tens of thousands of holiday-makers arrive in Scotland each year solely to pursue sporting activities. Facilities are excellent for a great range of more-or-less warm weather sports, and in recent winters skiing has been booming. Tour operators, Scottish centres and hotels offer package holidays for specific sports, or multi-sport programmes for the entire family.

Golf

Just as Scottish as whisky and probably healthier, golf is a powerful lure for visitors from around the world eager to play the game where it was devised. The surprise is that they can do it so cheaply and easily. And

Links Lineage

How long ago it got started in this chilly and windy land isn't clear, but in 1457 James II tried outlawing golf as a menace to national security: too many Scots marksmen were skipping their archery practice and swinging at a little ball instead. That ban didn't work, nor did several others. They say Mary Queen of Scots loved the game so much that she took to the fairways while in mourning for her husband, Darnley. She is thought to have played at Bruntsfield in Edinburgh, probably the oldest course on which golf is still played today. The earliest golf balls were made of leather stuffed with feathers. Not until 1901 was the rubber-cored ball invented. You'll see splendid old golf clubs dating back to the 17th century and other historical relics of the sport at the Spalding Golf Museum in Camperdown Park, Dundee.

84

by choosing your hotel or a special golf holiday arrangement with a bit of care, you can play a different course each day for a week or a fortnight. (See also pp. 114–15.)

St Andrews, for example, has 4 courses of its own, plus 11 more within easy reach in north-east Fife. They claim more golf courses per capita here than anywhere on earth. Visitors who yearn to play the historic Old Course at St Andrews' Royal and Ancient Golf Club, the home of golf, should either apply at least two months in advance or enter the daily "ballot", a lottery to determine which golfers will fill vacancies and cancellations the following day. Although St Andrews is jammed in summer and everyone wants to try the great Open Championship

Neither rain, nor snow, nor savage storms manage to keep the Scots at home, away from their golf courses.

links, daylight lingers far into the night so more people can tee off.

Other outstanding Scottish courses include Carnoustie, Royal Troon, Turnberry and Gleneagles.

Fishing

Scotland's rivers, lochs and off-shore deeps offer some of Europe's greatest game angling. Much of it is free or very cheap. You don't need a general fishing licence, just a local permit. Casting your line in the more highly prized salmon beats, on the other hand, costs hundreds of pounds per week—and for the privilege you may have to book a year ahead.

The Spey, Tay and Tweed are famous for salmon, sea trout and brown trout. But these fish also run in dozens of other Scottish waters. Most angling is fly; occasionally spinner or bait is permitted. If you'd like to learn the difference between a dry fly and an insect or how to stay upright while wading and casting in a rushing burn, there are experts all over Scotland. See p. 114 for more details.

Close season for trout is from October 7 to March 14, but in some places it's banned

for even longer; for salmon net fishing, it's from late August into February, for salmon rod fishing from some time in October until January or February. Coarse fishing, for such delights as perch and pike, is permitted year round and can be very good, particularly in southern waters.

Sea angling trips run from many ports along the Scottish coast and in the islands, or you can fish with good prospects from countless shoreline perches. Giant skate and halibut have been caught in the north. Such species as dogfish, mackerel, conger and pollack abound. Towards the end of summer you might well hook blue or porbeagle shark.

Boating and Wetter Water Sports

Hire a canoe, a dinghy, a sailing boat, a motor-cruiser or a yacht to explore Scotland's marvellous inland and coastal waters. Or, bring your own as thousands of boat enthusiasts do each summer. Sailing schools offer courses for beginners on lochs and around the western islands. Assuming you document your proficiency, you may charter larger craft without skipper; fully crewed boats are also available for hire. To get afloat in groups, try an organized cruise on Loch Lomond, the Clyde or Loch Ness.

On such placid waters as Loch Earn and Loch Tay you'll be able to water-ski, first learning how if necessary. Scotland has a certain number of days with very hot sunshine, and a great deal of swimming goes on—not all of it in the pools you find at resort towns. Officials warn about undertow or rip current off western coasts.

Scuba diving is growing in popularity in Scotland as in so many areas around the world. There are sub-aqua sites along the coast, in various inland lochs and around Mull and other islands. Tourist information centres have details.

Hill Walking and Mountain Climbing

The most stubborn indoor person should succumb to the lure of Scotland's landscape. In the Highlands, particularly, you'll find nature walks and hill or plateau excursions conducted by guides who know the terrain and are trained naturalists. There are even week-long hikes over moors and glens with food and accommodation included in the package price. At Glen Coe and Torridon, the

At centres around Scotland, ponies are waiting to take you on a trek.

National Trust for Scotland conducts especially fine and inexpensive guided walks.

Maps and guidebooks are available at information centres near many mountains popular with climbers, including the Cuillins on Skye and the peaked ridges of Arran. Despite an energetic safety campaign, significant numbers of climbers continue to get into trouble in Scotland, many having to be brought down by mountain rescue teams. Always get local advice on weather and conditions and plan your route to be back before dark. And never go alone.

Pony Trekking and Riding

All over Scotland there are horse and pony centres where you can ride by the hour, half-day or full day. Pony treks are normally led by expert guides and may be suitable for young children. Trail riding by horse, at a faster pace, is designed for experienced riders. Some centres offer accommodation and weekly package programmes with a different ride each day. It's a great way to explore the countryside.

Stalking and Shooting

To stalk any of those thousands of Scottish red deer you'll need a firearms certificate (from the area police headquarters where you'll shoot), a game licence (from a post office) and lots of money. Some hotels and guest houses have private stalking and shooting rights for their guests on nearby estates at daily rates justifying the common complaint that deer stalking is a "rich man's sport". Hunting

season for red deer stags is from July 1 to October 20, for grouse August 12 ("the glorious twelfth") to December 10.

Tennis, Bowls, Pitch and Put

A few of the more expensive countryside hotels feature tennis courts; Edinburgh has more than 100 public courts. You'll find bowling greens and pitch-and-put courses all over. Curling, which you could describe as bowls on ice, has been played in Scotland for at least 400 years.

Skiing

You'll find instructors, chair-lifts, tows and mushrooming accommodation at Scotland's three developed ski areas: Cairngorm, Glenshee and Glen Coe. Although weather can be severe, there's usually snow on the slopes from November into May.

Shopping

From the ubiquitous sheep come many of Scotland's finest and most famous products. But there are scores of other locally made items to tempt you, some of which you might consume before reaching home.

Shops are generally open 9 a.m.–5.30 p.m. Monday to Friday and on Saturday morning, if not all day. Be on the lookout for the "early closing" day, which varies from town to town, and within cities from district to district. It can be a minor inconvenience, when you don't know the system.

For major purchases, investigate the personal export scheme available from many stores, under which overseas visitors can avoid paying VAT (the sales tax included in prices). The shop undertakes either to ship your item to your home address or to have it delivered to your departing flight.

Better Buys

The range of Scottish **woollen items** seems endless. Aside from Shetland sweaters, scarves, skirts and suits you'll see sheepskin and woollen rugs, men's Highland evening wear (tartan kilt with Prince Charles or Jacobean dress jacket), Icelandic-style winter outer jackets with hoods, sheepskin slippers, seat covers and dusters. Many shops specialize in made-to-measure kilts. Harris tweed (from the Outer Hebri-

des) and cashmere are always best-sellers.

Deerskin is an unusual purchase, perhaps a large piece for hanging, or a tobacco pouch. Antlers aren't wasted: you'll find all kinds of things crafted from stag horns.

There are several major lines of **glassware** handmade in Scotland: Edinburgh and Stuart Crystal and Caithness Glass, with distinctive thistle or star designs.

The Scottish Craft Centre in Edinburgh's Royal Mile sells the best of Scotland's **craftwork.** Another selection is to be found at a Highlands and Islands centre in Inverness. Look for Highland **"heathergems",** jewellery fashioned from stems of heather. Heather is also used in soap and perfumes, as is Scottish seaweed. From the Orkney and Shetland islands you may see attractive **silvercraft** with designs inspired by Norse mythology. There is interesting **stoneware** and saltglazed **pottery** from the north, **glassware** from Oban. Hand-**painted stones** are decorative and inexpensive. Handsome **playing cards** with historical Scottish motifs seem almost too fancy to shuffle and deal. **Heraldic shields** with a crest and a patch of tartan denote your clan.

91

Bagpipes? There are half a dozen suppliers in Edinburgh alone.

Among Scottish **antiques,** duelling pistols are prized.

Highland oatcakes, Orkney and other fudges, pure butter shortbread, butterscotch and the amazing array of **Scottish sweets** may be memorable but hardly durable souvenirs. Edinburgh rock is a very sweet pink, white, lilac or orange stick. **Marmalade** from this land where it originated is an obvious choice: it even comes in whisky flavour.

Scotch whisky is probably no cheaper in Scotland, but you'll find far more brands than you ever thought existed. It's said that some of the best malts never leave the Highlands unless carried off by connoisseurs.

Nightlife

While sport addicts take advantage of Scotland's twilight-towards-midnight in the summer, the non-athletic will find a variety of indoor evening entertainment. The big cities offer the most, of course, but hotels around the countryside make sure tourists aren't bored.

Edinburgh has musical, literary and dramatic performances year round, although nothing matches the cultural concentration during the three-week **international festival** every August-September. Booking in advance for the "name" performers is essential.

Ceilidhs or **folk nights,** held frequently all over Scotland, feature dancers, pipers, fiddlers and other local or touring entertainers. Folk festivals are staged in such centres as Wick, Inverness and Kinross. You'll find **theatrical seasons** in Pitlochry, Mull, St Andrews, Braemar and Oban, an international festival of youth orchestras in Aberdeen, a drama-cinema-music season in Stirling, a Robert Burns festival in Burns Country, a season of Proms in Glasgow.

The capital's **discotheques,** striving gamely to keep abreast of the latest musical frenzies, may stay open as late as 3 or 4 in the morning on weekends.

The **film** scene apart from the Edinburgh festival will not excite many visitors, but there are cinemas in many towns.

With few exceptions, **pubs** in Scotland single-mindedly concentrate on liquid consumption: don't expect the atmosphere or diversions often found in English pubs.

Dining and Drinking

Not the least of Scotland's many surprises is how much good cooking you find, even in remote spots. It will usually cost more than the standard uninspiring fare too often churned out for tourists here as elsewhere in the United Kingdom, but the quality of the cuisine and of the Scottish liquid refreshment should ease the pain.

Better chefs make full if not often elaborate use of the grand local basics: fresh salmon and trout, herring, beef, venison, grouse, pheasant, potatoes, raspberries and other fruits. And, of course, oatmeal which turns up in all manner of dishes. Samuel Johnson's opinion of oats after he toured the northern regions is still much quoted: "A grain which in England is generally given to horses, but in Scotland supports the people." You'll be glad it does, after sampling oatmeal porridge, oatcakes and oatmeal coating on such things as herring and cheese.

Much Scottish fare is hearty, which helps fortify one against the weather. Whenever you can, try traditional dishes—not **93** as exotic as their names sometimes suggest and often delicious. To find restaurants that serve the local specialities, look for a stockpot sign or consult the Scottish Tourist Board's list of establishments participating in the "Taste of Scotland" programme.

Places and Prices
While you won't have to search for breakfast, which is provided abundantly by almost every hotel and guest house in Scotland, restaurants, roadside inns and snack bars are rather thin on the ground. If you're touring, consider picnic lunches—there's no shortage of lovely sites. For evening meals, most of the finest Scottish restaurants away from the cities are in hotels; they usually serve non-residents, but in summer be sure to book.

Meal hours: You may not be served lunch before 12.30 or much after 2 p.m. or dinner before 7 or after 9 p.m., in restaurants away from major centres. High tea, often a meal itself, is usually served between 4.30 and 6.30 p.m.

In general, restaurant prices compare favourably to those south of the border—which does not prevent certain Scottish establishments, flushed with published accolades and perhaps conscious of the shortness of the "season", from charging prices depressingly familiar to diners in London's West End. The 15 per cent VAT (sales tax included in prices) and a frequent 10 per cent service charge don't help either.

Breakfast—and Smoked Fish
The Scottish breakfast, usually included in your overnight rate, is often better than the English. Oatmeal porridge here is made with salt and served with cream or milk (sugar is severely frowned upon) and, Scotland being Scotland, it's a welcome hot starter in summer

Perhaps stretching your budget, try at least one Scottish country-house restaurant where dining can be sophisticated—and delicious.

as well as winter. Aside from regular features like fruit juice, fresh fruit, eggs, sausage, bacon, toast (not hot any more often than in England), morning rolls (which *should* be hot), jams and marmalade, the Scottish kipper adds something very special to breakfast. It's hard to argue with conventional wisdom that Loch Fyne kippers are best, but it's just as hard to find a smoked herring from anywhere in Scotland that isn't delicious.

Smoked fish specialities, dating back to Norse days, appeal to many people at any meal. Famous Arbroath smokies are salted haddock flavoured by hot birch or oak smoke. Finnan haddock (or haddie) are salted and smoked over peat. Patés of kippers, smoked salmon, trout and haddock have become favourite starters in good restaurants. They are often superb, as is a smoked haddock omelet.

Soups

Enormously popular year round, traditional Scottish soups are of course best homemade. Recipes vary. Worth trying:

Cock-a-leekie—a seasoned broth from boiling fowl with leeks and at times onions and prunes, consumed for at least 400 years and dubbed the national soup of Scotland.

Partan bree—cream crab (partan) soup.

Scotch broth—multi-vegetable, barley-thickened soup with mutton or beef.

Cullen skink—milky broth of Finnan haddock with onions and potatoes.

Lorraine soup—chicken cream soup with almonds, nutmeg and lemon, named after (if not brought over by) Mary of Guise-Lorraine, mother of Mary Queen of Scots.

Oatmeal soup—creamed, with onion, leek, carrot and turnip.

Main Courses

Salmon, prince of Scotland's lochs and rivers, is preferred simmered (never boiled) and served either hot with hollandaise sauce or cold with mayonnaise. Salmon trout, which tastes more of salmon than trout, is often baked and served with hollandaise. Trout itself may be grilled, fried or poached, with lemon the usual garnish. These typical Scottish **fish,** and a variety of white fish, lobster and other shellfish caught in the sea, have risen quite sharply in price in recent years: they now often cost more than meat in a restaurant.

Game still abounds in Scotland, so much so that a good deal is exported to the Continent. After the "glorious 12th" of August when the shooting season begins, grouse is a pricey but much-sought menu item, served roasted or in a pie. It's best after being hung for a week or two. With some 300,000 red deer at large, venison frequently appears in restaurants, as roast most often or in casserole. You'll also find pheasant, guinea fowl, quail and hare. Terrines and patés of game are popular, as are hashes and game pies.

Scottish **beef** (another major export item), rivals Europe's best. Whisky goes into various sauces served with it, including Gaelic steak, which is seasoned with garlic and fried in sauteed onions with whisky poured on during the process. Whisky is also used in preparing seafood, poultry and game. Forfar bridies, another traditional dish, consist of pastry puffs stuffed with minced steak and onions (reminiscent of Cornish pasties). If you're lucky, you might find beef collops in pickled walnut sauce. Veal is rather rare. Lamb doesn't appear on menus as often as you'd expect, considering the vast acreage given over to ovine pasturage. When it does, it may be ragout, chops or roast.

Haggis hardly deserves its horrific reputation among squeamish non-Scots. Properly, it consists of chopped fresh sheep's innards, oatmeal, onions, beef suet and seasoning, boiled inside a sewn-up sheep's stomach bag. Scottish associations around the world serve haggis for their January 25 "Burns Night" celebrations. With haggis you should be served chappit tatties and bashed neeps—mashed potatoes and turnips. A powerful Scottish school of thought insists that whisky should accompany haggis.

Potatoes are a particular local pride. There's much ado about stovies, sliced potatoes and onions stewed together, sometimes with meat scraps. Rumbledethumps are a mixture of boiled cabbage and mashed potatoes, possibly with onions or chives and grated cheese. You shouldn't have to go all the way to northernmost Caithness for its basic dish of tatties (potatoes boiled in their jackets) and herrings. And in the Orkneys with their haggis they like clapshot—boiled potatoes and turnips mashed together and seasoned with fresh black pepper. **97**

Snacks, Teas, Cheese and Sweets

At its best, home-made wholemeal bread is a crusty, sandy-coloured delight. Scones, bannocks, pancakes, baps and shortbread are among the great array of Scottish **baked and girdled goods.** Oatcakes, the best known, come either rough or smooth (those with coarser texture have more character), and you'll see them eaten on their own or with butter, paté, jam or crowdie, Scotland's centuries-old version of cottage cheese.

Scotch **eggs** are deep-fried, sausage-coated hard-boiled eggs eaten hot or cold, often with salad. Scotch woodcock usually involves pieces of toast covered with anchovy and scrambled egg.

Caboc, a mild Highland cream **cheese** wrapped in oatmeal, appears all over, even in souvenir shops. Hramsa is another Highland cream cheese with herbs and wild garlic, which school children are sent out to pick. Year-old white Mclelland and one- or two-year-old white Dalbeattie are distinguished Scottish cheddars, but not easy to find. Red, white and smoked Orkney cheeses are often served; none is especially tangy. White Stuart crumbles. Blue Stuart bites a bit. Scotland's best blue, Caledonian, is not produced commercially but your restaurateur may have a connection.

For **dessert,** you'll see various combinations of cheese with red berries or black cherries and vanilla ice. Cranachan, a tasty Scottish speciality however differently chefs prepare it, usually consists of toasted oatmeal, cream, rum or whisky, nuts and raspberries or other soft fruit. Rhubarb and ginger tart is worth watching for. Dundee, birthplace of modern bitter-orange marmalade, also contributes a popular fruit cake and a crumble.

As for whisky, you might find it in your sliced oranges, halved peaches, chocolate mousse, sponge cake or soufflé.

Beverages

Graciously, Scotland permits other alcoholic drinks apart from whisky to be sold within its borders. Licensed restaurants have **wine** cellars, although the selection is often limited. It is not easy to find French-bottled claret (Bordeaux) or burgundy, since most Scottish hotels and restaurants take their wines from large importers who bottle primarily in Britain. You may also see a few not overly distinguished German, Italian, Spanish and Portuguese wines. Almost always there will be a relatively inexpensive house red and white available by the glass or carafe.

Scotland is proud of its own **beers** which, visitors are surprised to find, do not include an equivalent of English "bitter". The "half and a half" featured in any old-fashioned pub is a dram of whisky with a half-pint of beer as a chaser.

A tremendous amount of lore, some say mumbo-jumbo, attends the entire saga of **Scotch whisky,** from its distillation involving pure mountain water, the aroma of peat and five centuries of expertise all the way to the actual drinking.

Scots are likely to seize on any occasion for a wee toast. Cheers!

But there's no question that—despite many attempts at imitation—there is only one true Scotch whisky.

The word whisky derives from the Gaelic *uisge beatha*, water of life. It comes in two basic types: malt, distilled solely from malted barley, and grain whisky from malted barley and grain. Most of the Scotch sold today is blended, combining malt and grain whiskies. Straight malt whisky, somewhat sturdier stuff primarily from the Highlands, has always been a local favourite and recently has been gaining adherents worldwide. There are more than 2,000 brands of authentic Scotch.

Purists insist that single malt whisky should be drunk only neat or with plain water—never with soda, lemonade or ginger ale, which are quite often mixed with *blended* Scotch even by Scots.

There is also a sizeable body of Scottish opinion which holds that while Scotch whisky in moderation is definitely healthy and should always be kept handy, it is not necessary to drink it before or during breakfast.

After dinner, Scotland's version of Irish coffee, naturally using local whisky, may be called a "tartan" or a "Gaelic".

A "rusty nail", thought for obvious reasons to have associations with a coffin nail, is one measure of malt whisky and one measure of Drambuie. The even more devastating "earthquake" contains one-third whisky, one-third gin and one-third absinth. A "Scotch mist" in Scotland is whisky, squeezed lemon rind and crushed ice, shaken well. An "Atholl brose" blends oatmeal, heather honey and whisky.

Mineral water, still or effervescent, is slowly making inroads into the Scottish refreshment scene. You'll find Scottish and French brands.

Coffees and **teas** in Scotland are similar to what is available in England. Continental coffee is hard to find away from the major centres.

Note: Because of a recent relaxation of the drinking laws in Scotland, you'll find certain licensed premises open from 11 a.m. to 11 p.m. without the mandatory afternoon closure common to England. Most pubs, which are rather more down-to-earth than their English counterparts, are still closed on Sundays. But hotel bars may be open: if so, they'll advertise their 7-day licence. Those under 18 are not allowed to drink in licensed premises.

Great Scots

Robert Adam (1728–92): architect, designed the best of Edinburgh's New Town, Culzean Castle and other leading Scottish buildings.

John Logie Baird (1888–1946): scientist acclaimed here as the "inventor of television" since he was the first to transmit TV over a distance.

Sir James Barrie (1860–1937): dramatist, novelist, wrote *Peter Pan.*

James Boswell (1740–95): biographer of Samuel Johnson.

James Bruce (1730–94): explorer, discovered source of Blue Nile.

Robert Burns (1759–96): Scotland's leading poet and song writer, wrote "Tam o' Shanter" and "Auld Lang Syne".

Thomas Carlyle (1795–1881): historian, rewrote classic *French Revolution* after first draft was accidentally burnt.

Alexander Fleming (1881–1955): bacteriologist, discovered penicillin.

David Hume (1711–76): philosopher, historian, wrote *An Enquiry Concerning Human Nature.*

Lord William Thompson Kelvin (1824–1907): scientist, pioneered trans-Atlantic telegraphy, developed theory of tides.

John Knox (1505–72): leader of Scotland's Protestant Reformation.

David Livingstone (1813–73): missionary explorer, mapped Zambesi River, lakes and much of African interior.

John L. McAdam (1756–1836): engineer whose waterproof road surface bears his name.

John Napier (1550–1617): mathematician, discovered logarithms.

Sir Henry Raeburn (1756–1823): dominant portrait painter of his age.

Sir Walter Scott (1771–1832): romantic poet ("The Lady of the Lake"), novelist *(Waverley, Rob Roy),* Scottish patriot-publicist.

Sir James Simpson (1811–70): medical scientist, pioneered use of chloroform as anesthesia in surgery.

Adam Smith (1723–90): scholar, founded science of political economy, wrote *The Wealth of Nations.*

Robert Louis Stevenson (1850–94): novelist, essayist, poet, wrote *Treasure Island, The Strange Case of Dr Jekyll and Mr Hyde.*

Robert William Thompson (1822–73): inventor of first pneumatic rubber tire.

James Watt (1736–1819): inventor of modern condensing steam engine.

BLUEPRINT for a Perfect Trip

How to Get There

From North America

BY AIR: Scotland is easily accessible by air from the United States via three principal cities: Aberdeen, Glasgow and Edinburgh. There are direct flights daily between Boston, Montreal, New York and Prestwick, and connecting flights from many U.S. and Canadian cities.

The new "open-skies" policy allows transatlantic flights to Glasgow—ending the monopoly of Prestwick Airport.

Visitors from abroad interested in touring by rail may buy a **Britrail Pass,** a flat-rate unlimited-use ticket. This *cannot* be purchased within Britain.

Charter Flights and Package Tours. Most GIT's (Group Inclusive Tours), one to three weeks, to Scotland's principal cities, feature sights in England as well as in major cities on the Continent. Included in the GIT are round-trip air transport, hotel accommodation, some meals and sightseeing. There are some charter flights to Prestwick from New York, Detroit and Chicago.

From England and Eire

BY AIR: There is direct service from all parts of the U.K. to Scotland, including frequent departures from Birmingham, London and Manchester. There are also regular flights from Cork, Shannon and Dublin. The Irish routes all have economy fares, APEX fares and an excursion fare. There is a special night excursion fare from Belfast to Glasgow.

Package Tours: There is an amazing array of package holidays to be had in Scotland, from full board in a comfortable hotel with sightseeing trips, to more budget-minded arrangements which can include travel by air/rail to the hotel. You can choose among self-catering accommodation, guest houses, or staying in a "centre" (if holidays with a theme appeal to you). Reasonably priced "weekend breaks" are another possibility.

BY RAIL: Tourists may take advantage of several special fares. The **Travelpass** gives unlimited travel on most train, bus and boat facilities in the Highlands and islands.

If you fancy having your car with you in Scotland but don't relish the long drive up, consider shipping your car on **Motorail** as far as Edinburgh. Not cheap, but a better deal than going by train and hiring a car there.

BY ROAD: Several major thoroughfares (such as the M6) go up to Scotland, as well as some scenic routes. Driving up the west coast of Scotland can be a little hazardous, as many of the roads are quite narrow.

BY COACH: There are frequent tour departures from all over the country to various Scottish destinations.

BY SEA: There are ferries from Northern Ireland to Ardrossan and Stranraer. The Isle of Arran ferry goes to Ardrossan, and there is ferry service between Aberdeen and Lerwick, Scrabster and Stromness. There also are, of course, many domestic ferries between the islands and from the mainland to the Western Isles (e.g. Kennacraig to Islay, Oban to Mull, Mallaig and Kyle of Lochalsh to Skye, Kyle of Lochalsh to Stornoway).

When to Go

The best months to visit Scotland are May and June which have the most hours of sunshine and comparatively little rain. The far north enjoys as many as 20 hours of daylight per day in June, and there aren't many of the midges and other stinging insects which become a problem in the full summer. September and early October are beautiful, but they'll be wetter.

Average monthly temperature in Edinburgh:

	J	F	M	A	M	J	J	A	S	O	N	D
Temperature F°	38	38	41	45	50	56	59	58	54	48	42	32
C°	3	3	4	7	10	13	15	14	12	9	6	4
Rainfall (inches)	2.8	2.2	2.0	1.7	2.6	2.0	3.2	3.3	2.7	3.3	2.9	2.4

Planning Your Budget

Though good value for money is still the rule in most cases in Scotland, bargains are rare, and inflation relentlessly works its familiar miseries.

Accommodation. *Double hotel room* with bath and breakfast £15–25 per person. *Guest house* (without private bath) £12–15 per person. *Bed & Breakfast* premises (without bath) £10–12 per person. *Youth hostel* £2.90–5.20 (breakfast £2.00).

Airports. *Edinburgh:* bus £2, taxi £10. *Glasgow:* bus £1.20, taxi £7. *Prestwick:* airline bus to Glasgow £3, to Edinburgh £4.

Babysitters. £1.50 per hour (£2 after midnight).

Bicycle hire. £5–8 per day, £25–35 per week.

Buses. Edinburgh to Glasgow £2.70 (£3.60 return), Glasgow to Portree (Skye) £15.60 (£20.30 return). City buses in Edinburgh about 30–50p.

Camping. £8–10 for a family of 4 (including 2 children) for one night.

Car hire (international company). *Ford Fiesta* £18 per day, plus insurance (VAT included), or £110 per week, insurance and VAT included, with unlimited mileage. *Audi 80* £22–25 per day, plus insurance and VAT, or £150 per week including insurance and VAT, with unlimited mileage.

Discotheque entry (Edinburgh). £2.50–7.00 (about £4 average).

Hairdressers. *Woman's* shampoo and set £6, shampoo, cut and set or blow-dry £13, permanent wave £25. *Man's* shampoo, cut and blow-dry £5.

Meals and drinks. Pub or café lunch £3, restaurant meal with wine £12, pint of beer £1.20, tot of whisky £1.

Newspapers. British dailies up to 30p. Financial Times 50p, International Herald Tribune 70p.

Shopping. Pure wool tartan £10 per metre, tweed £10–70 per metre, wool kilt skirt £25 (long £35), Fairisle sweaters £25, lambswool sweaters £70.

Sights. Most museums are free. Castles and gardens, £1–3.

Taxis. Basic rate 80p (for 670 yds.), plus £1 every mile.

Trains (2nd class return). Edinburgh to Inverness £19.50 (£22 Friday), Glasgow to Wick £24.80 (£27.60 Friday), London to Edinburgh £53 (£63 Friday) depending on day of travel. Freedom of Scotland 7-day train pass £46, 14-day £77.

An A–Z Summary of Practical Information and Facts

> A star (*) after an entry title indicates that prices concerning this section can be found on page 105.
>
> The information contained may be familiar to U.K. residents, but is intended to be of help to visitors from overseas.

A   **AIRPORTS*.** Scotland has four major airports—Edinburgh, Prestwick, Glasgow and Aberdeen—and some 25 minor airfields scattered about on the mainland and the islands.

Edinburgh airport is linked with the Waverley Bridge terminal in the centre of Edinburgh, 9 miles away, by an airline bus which leaves every half hour and takes about 30 minutes. Taxis are available just outside the arrival hall. At this busy, modern airport, you'll find porters and baggage trolleys, car-hire desks, a bank, an information desk, direct-line reservation phones to certain Edinburgh hotels, accommodation service at the Scottish Tourist Board, emergency medical and disabled travellers' facilities, a nursery, restaurants and bars, general and souvenir shops, and inside the international departure lounge, duty-free counters.

Prestwick airport, about one hour from Glasgow (28 miles), handles all of Scotland's long-haul inter-continental air traffic. This modern terminal, with public bus, train and taxi service to Glasgow and points in Ayrshire, has all the facilities you'll find at Edinburgh plus a complete duty-free supermarket and gift shop. Prestwick boasts that it has less fog than any airport in Europe—fewer than 11 hours per year.

Glasgow airport at Abbotsinch, a 9-mile, 20-minute taxi or bus ride (leaving every 20–30 minutes from Anderston Cross bus station), has all the usual facilities.

Aberdeen airport, a 7-mile, 35-minute bus or taxi ride from the Aberdeen railway station, also has modern facilities plus a nearby (North Sea oil-inspired) heliport.

Scotland's other airfields are served by Loganair, the Scottish domestic airline.

B   **BABYSITTERS*.** Hotels, guest houses and bed and breakfast premises around Scotland often provide babysitters, usually off-duty maids or students. In Edinburgh, the central tourist information bureau (see TOURIST INFORMATION) keeps a list of nannies and students in the city who babysit, and elsewhere local tourist offices will know someone.

BICYCLE HIRE*. Information offices at many tourist resorts in Scotland will direct you to local firms (or individuals) from which you can hire a cycle by the hour, day or week. The Scottish Tourist Board (see TOURIST INFORMATION) issues a free pamphlet listing many rental firms. You're advised to write ahead for a cycle if you're holidaying in July or August. Almost nowhere are there mopeds for hire.

CAMPING and CARAVANNING*. There are more than 600 campsites in Scotland for the growing number of visitors who come here to avoid living within four walls during their holiday. The most elaborate have hot showers, shaver points, flush toilets, laundry facilities, shops, tea rooms, and can offer nature trails, forest walks and even access to golf courses. Many sites are much more limited, with just a handful of pitches. A few of the most attractive locations are operated by the Forestry Commission, which describes them in a free leaflet (see below).

Within Edinburgh's city limits there are three sites, and five others are close enough for easy access. There are also several at Loch Lomond, within easy reach of Glasgow. To camp or caravan on private land, you need the owner's permission. Without it you may be prosecuted under the Trespass (Scotland) Act, 1865.

Write to your nearest BTA (British Tourist Authority) office (see TOURIST INFORMATION) for the booklet *Scotland: Caravan and Camping Sites*, or to

Information Branch, Forestry Commission, 231 Corstophine Road, Edinburgh EH12 7AT, for *Forestry Commission Camping and Caravan Sites*.

CAR HIRE*. As a rule, to hire a car from one of the many local and international firms you must be 21 years of age and have held a driving licence for at least 12 months. Virtually all the world's driving licences are recognized by the British authorities.

CHILDREN'S ACTIVITIES. There's no shortage of amusing things for children to see and do in Scotland. When they tire of stone-age relics, spooky castles and the search for prehistoric monsters, you might consider some of the following:

C In Edinburgh, the Museum of Childhood and the Wax Museum can be visited on a rainy day, and the zoo is always a favourite. If you're in Glasgow, there's the Museum of Transport (see p. 69—adults can combine it with a visit to the city's Art Gallery and Museum, close by) and Haggs Castle, which has a history museum for children.

To see the animals of Scotland in their natural surroundings, visit one of the numerous natural reserves. Three outstanding ones: the Highland Wildlife Park near Aviemore (see p. 61), the Loch of the Lowes near Dunkeld (see p. 46), and the bird sanctuary of Handa Island (see p. 64).

Pony trekking is a big hit with most youngsters. You can make arrangements for half- or full-day promenades through the countryside in popular areas like the Trossachs, Aberfoyle in Scotland's Central region, the Borders, around Aviemore and on the islands of Arran and Skye. (See also p. 88.)

And don't forget the Highland Games, colourful spectacles with lots of side shows (see p. 82).

The Scottish Tourist Board publishes an entertaining and informative brochure entitled *Scotland for Children.*

CIGARETTES, CIGARS, TOBACCO. If you're a smoker, take full advantage of your tax-free allowance on your journey here (see ENTRY FORMALITIES AND CUSTOMS). The prices of tobacco products in Britain are among the highest in the world. American and other foreign brands are even more expensive. Since most brands are sold both in packets of 10 and 20, you must specify the quantity when you buy.

British and a handful of European cigarette brands are available everywhere. Major centres have a greater selection of international tobacco products.

"Thank you for not smoking" is becoming a sign of the times. You'll see it in indoor tourist attractions like castles and museums, and in many hotel restaurants. All buses have seats for non-smokers. Outdoors you're urged to be extremely careful with matches, cigarette butts and pipe embers—a great deal of Scotland's landscape is ruinously disfigured by fire each year.

CLOTHING*. Even if you're holidaying in Scotland in mid-summer, take warm clothing and rain wear. Anoraks are very useful: buy a bright colour to warn hunters if you'll be hiking or climbing. Sturdy shoes are a must. In more expensive hotels, men will not feel comfortable at dinner without a jacket and probably a tie, though well-heeled golfers and anglers sometimes get away with less formal attire.

Scotland makes some of the world's best clothing, and you'll find a very good selection of woollens, tartans and tweeds, although not at significantly lower prices than elsewhere in the United Kingdom.

Following is a comparison of British and American sizes. Remember however that clothing size may vary according to manufacturers. Men's suit and shirt sizes are the same in the U.S. and Britain.

Women's clothes					
Great Britain	10/32	12/34	14/36	16/38	18/40
U.S.A.	8/32	10/34	12/36	14/38	16/40
Women's footwear					
Great Britain	3	4	5	6	7
U.S.A.	$4\frac{1}{2}$	$5\frac{1}{2}$	$6\frac{1}{2}$	$7\frac{1}{2}$	$8\frac{1}{2}$
Men's footwear					
Great Britain	6	7	8	9	10
U.S.A.	$6\frac{1}{2}$	$7\frac{1}{2}$	$8\frac{1}{2}$	$9\frac{1}{2}$	$10\frac{1}{2}$

COMMUNICATIONS

Post offices and mail. The United Kingdom offers first- and second-class mail service for letters and packets. In view of the occasional delays by second-class mail, it's advisable to pay the modest extra postage and send mail within Britain by first class. Postcards and letters to Europe and other points overseas automatically go airmail.

Stamps are sold at post offices (found in almost every Scottish village even if they share space with grocery shops) and newsagents, as well as vending machines. You may be given Scottish or English stamps, both valid throughout the United Kingdom.

If you're not sure which hotel you'll be staying in, you can receive mail c/o Poste Restante or simply c/o Post Office in the town. You'll need a passport, driving licence or other official identification to pick up mail. There's no charge.

Telegrams no longer exist in Scotland. Inland telegrams have been replaced by Telemessages, dictated over the telephone, Monday to Saturday, with following day delivery.

C **Telephone***. Public coin phones are located in post offices or red or blue booths in the street. You'll also find them in pubs, restaurants and other public buildings. The amount of privacy you'll have varies with the location. Red telephone boxes and other public coin phones take 5p and 10p coins. Blue payphones operate with 2p, 5p, 10p and 50p coins to facilitate international phone calls. Payphones with one single slot also accept 20p and £1 coins. Information on overseas dialling codes and the international exchange is clearly displayed. To make a "collect" call, ask the operator to "reverse the charges".

From October to May, information on skiing conditions in Scotland is transmitted on the Ski Hotline—telephone 0898 654654. For weather conditions in south and southwest Scotland, dial 031-246 8091.

COMPLAINTS. The local tourist office and/or the Scottish Tourist Board in Edinburgh will want to know of any complaint you have which the owner or manager of the establishment in question has not resolved to your satisfaction. For appropriate matters, contact the police.

In Great Britain, consumer protection enjoys legal backing. If an article doesn't correspond to its description, or is defective, you may always return it (providing you've kept the sales receipt). Since the law is on your side, you'll have no trouble from the shop-owner. Proprietors may offer you a voucher for the amount in question, but you have the right to insist on a cash refund.

CONSULATES. All the embassies are located in London, but many countries maintain consulates in Scotland. Check their hours first by phone.

Australia: 80 Hanover St., Edinburgh EH2 2HQ, tel. 031-226 6271

Canada: 151 St. Vincent St., Glasgow G2 5NJ, tel. 041-248 5011

South Africa: Stock Exchange House, Glasgow G2 1BX, tel. 041-221 3114

U.S.A.: 3 Regent Terrace, Edinburgh EH7 5BW, tel. 031-556 8315

CONVERTER CHARTS. For fluid and distance measures, see page

112.

Weight

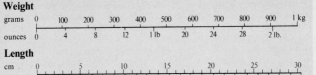

Length

CRIME and THEFT. Low by world standards, the crime rate in Scotland is unfortunately rising. Police warn that theft, particularly involving cars and usually caused by carelessness, spoils too many holidays. In hotels, put your most valuable objects in the safe and never leave important possessions in evidence. If you're caravanning, lock up before walking off, and don't leave radios, handbags, etc. near open windows even when you're right there.

DRIVING IN SCOTLAND. Arriving with your own or a hired car, you'll need registration and insurance papers and a driving licence. Seat belts are required by law.

Driving conditions. Police say an increasing number of foreign motorists get involved in road accidents in Scotland, often because they forget to drive on the left. But in the hinterland, driving can be a challenge even to British motorists. Many of the twisting and humpbacked secondary roads are single-track, with passing places into which you're expected to swing to make way for an oncoming car, or to allow a faster car behind you to overtake. Although there are usually enough passing places along these narrow stretches, when traffic is heavy progress is agonizingly slow as you pull into and out of the side-slips. The form is to wave at the other driver if he pulls off for you. Obviously, you should never park in these essential passing places, even briefly to admire the scenery. Other obstacles include sheep and cattle, on minor roads, and farm vehicles which you may encounter on any Scottish road except the limited motorways (expressways) in the central area. Signposting is generally excellent, but you'll need a good map.

Speed limits. In built-up areas, 30 or 40 mph; on major roads 60 mph; on motorways (expressways) 70 mph.

Parking. There are meters in major centres and vigilant corps of traffic police and wardens to ticket violators, even in small towns. Meters take 20p pieces, ticket machines up to 50p.

Fuel and oil. Petrol is sold by the Imperial gallon (about 10% more voluminous than the U.S. gallon) and by the litre, both registering at the pumps. Four-star grade is 97 octane; three-star 94 octane. Unleaded petrol is widely available. The majority of petrol stations are self-service. In the more remote areas, stations are rather scarce but you'll appreciate the friendly service when you find one.

Fluid measures

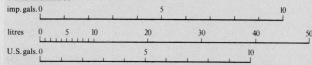

Distance

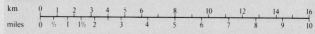

Repairs. Most centres have at least one garage for car repairs, often very crowded during the summer. Automobile club members affiliated with the British Automobile Association (AA) or the Royal Automobile Club (RAC) can take advantage of speedy, efficient assistance in case of a breakdown.

RAC Rescue Service throughout Scotland: tel. 031-228 3911.

Drinking and driving. If you plan to drink more than a sip of whisky or half a pint of beer you'd better leave the car behind. Penalties are severe, involving loss of licence, heavy fines and even prison sentences; and the law is strictly applied.

Road signs. Many standard international picture signs are displayed in Scotland. Some visiting motorists may take a while to get used to the arrows and other signs on country road surfaces in (sometimes fading) white paint; these may or may not be accompanied by regular road signs. Usefully, signs announcing your arrival in towns often indicate the number of miles to the next one along the road and from the town you've just left. Some written signs may perplex Americans:

British	American
Carriageway	Roadway; traffic lane
Clearway	No parking along highway
Diversion	Detour
Dual carriageway	Divided highway
Give way	Yield
Level crossing	Railroad crossing
Motorway	Expressway
No overtaking	No passing
Roadworks	Men working
Roundabout	Traffic circle

ELECTRIC CURRENT. Throughout Scotland it's 240 volts A.C., 50 cycles. Certain appliances may need a converter. At the very least Americans will need an adaptor for British sockets, which come in a variety of sizes.

EMERGENCIES. For fire brigade, police, ambulance, coast guard, lifeboat or mountain rescue service, dial 999 from any telephone. You need no coin. Tell the emergency operator which service you need. See also individual entries such as CONSULATES and MEDICAL CARE.

ENTRY FORMALITIES and CUSTOMS. For non-British citizens, the same formalities apply at Scottish ports of entry as elsewhere in the United Kingdom. Citizens of most Commonwealth countries require a visa; check with your travel agent before departure. In many other cases travellers need only a valid passport, filling out a brief immigration form to enter for a tourist visit. More and more North Americans heading for holidays in Scotland are flying direct to Prestwick where customs and immigration delays are far shorter than at London's Heathrow.

In British ports and airports if you have goods to declare you follow a red channel; with nothing to declare you take the green route, bypassing inspection. But customs officers look over the faces of green-channel travellers and uncannily choose certain tourists to check. Being caught in the green channel smuggling anything at all, even an extra carton of cigarettes, is no laughing matter, for the British sense of honour is offended.

The following chart shows the main duty-free items you may take into Britain and, when returning home, into your own country:

113

E

Into:	Cigarettes	Cigars	Tobacco	Spirits	Wine
Britain*	400 or	100 or	500 g.	1 l. and	2 l.
Australia	200 or	250 g. or	250 g.	1 l. or	1 l.
Canada	200 and	50 and	900 g.	1.1 l. or	1.1 l.
Eire	200 or	50 or	250 g.	1 l. and	2 l.
N. Zealand	200 or	50 or	250 g.	1.1 l. and	4.5 l.
S. Africa	400 and	50 and	250 g.	1 l. and	2 l.
U.S.A.	200 and	100 and	**	1 l. or	1 l.

* For non-European residents. (Coming from Eire: 200 cigarettes,
50 cigars, 250 g. tobacco).
** A reasonable amount for personal use.

Currency restrictions. There's no limit on the amount of pounds or foreign currency you can bring into or take out of Great Britain. Check to see whether your own country has any regulations on import and export of currency.

F **FISHING.** To take advantage of Scotland's superb fishing possibilities, you need only a permit for the particular area. Some hotels have fishing rights, others will arrange this for you. Or you may prefer a package fishing holiday with instruction, equipment and tackle included. Angling—except for salmon—is surprisingly inexpensive.

The Scottish Tourist Board's publications like *Scotland for Fishing* and *Angling in the Scottish Borders* will fill you in on the best spots, seasons, permits and so on.

G **GOLF.** Scotland has more than 400 golf courses where visitors may play. Many welcome visiting players with no more formality than modest greens fees and perhaps, a letter from the home club. Some private clubs limit unaccompanied visitors to week days and certain hours. You can hire clubs, caddies or golf trolleys (no golf carts).

Scotland, Home of Golf is a comprehensive booklet published and sold by the Scottish Tourist Board. It lists courses and clubs where visitors are welcome, with charges and restrictions, as well as details of festivals and package holidays (including accommodation, fees and lessons for those who are interested).

Open competitions in which visitors may participate are listed in *Events in Scotland*, available free from the Scottish Tourist Board.

GUIDES. Address enquiries to The Secretary, Scottish Tourist Guides Association, 5 Duddingston Road, Edinburgh EH15 1ND, tel. 031-661 6038.

Members of this professional guides association wear official badges engraved with their names. Most are based in Edinburgh or Glasgow. Some will travel. Rates are by the half or full day. Some transport companies employ their own guides. During the summer you may find university students free-lancing as guides.

HAIRDRESSERS and BARBERS*. You'll have no trouble finding a place to have your hair cut, shampooed, blow-dried or permed in towns around Scotland. You may have to do it co-ed: as elsewhere in Europe, unisex salons have become fashionable. Tip around 10%.

HITCH-HIKING. Safe, popular and legal everywhere in Scotland—except on motorways (expressways), where you are liable to a fine. You can position yourself on an approach road to a motorway and thumb, but stay off the highway itself. You're more likely to get a lift in a country area than on major routes.

HOTELS and ACCOMMODATION*. More than 3,300 hotels and 7,000 guest houses and bed and breakfast premises offer holiday accommodation. The Scottish Tourist Board (see TOURIST INFORMATION) lists many of these establishments in inexpensive booklets, recommends minimum standards but carries out no inspections. In addition there are many hundreds of self-catering cottages, stationary caravans, chalets, farmhouses, lodges, croft houses (small farms) and flats to let.

Book ahead for Easter, July and August if at all possible. If not, most tourist offices offer "Local Bed-Booking" and "Book-a-Bed-Ahead" services which assure you of overnight accommodation on the same day. For this reservation you pay the tourist bureau a minimal deposit, which is deducted from your bill.

Hotels range from basic to top international standard. Many of the most pleasant are converted country mansions in isolated settings. Rooms with private bathrooms exist but are by no means the general rule in Scottish hotels. On the other hand, some 60 hotels have swimming pools and about 20 have their own golf courses.

H   In a Scottish hotel, as throughout Britain, you simply sign your name to register. On departure, your bill includes Value Added Tax (VAT) and sometimes a service charge which is otherwise left to "your discretion" (10% is about as discreet as you'll want to be).

The Scottish Tourist Board (STB) lists a great many hotels which have special facilities for disabled visitors and young children, and which offer low-season prices for senior citizens.

Guest houses and **Bed and Breakfast (B&B)** premises can be great bargains, though you'll rarely have a private bathroom. Rooms in almost all hotels, guest houses and bed and breakfast places have hot and cold running water. More and more establishments of all categories are serving an evening meal or high tea.

Youth Hostels. The Scottish Youth Hostels Association maintains 80 hostels in Scotland open to anyone over the age of 5 who has a national or international membership card. Facilities and regulations vary. Their address is:

7 Glebe Crescent, Stirling FK8 2JA, tel. 0786 51181.

HOURS

Banks. 9.30 a.m.–12.30 p.m., 1.30–3.30 p.m., Monday to Friday, plus a 4.30–6 p.m. extension on Thursday in major centres and possibly during lunchtime on Friday. Airport bank-currency exchange offices operate for longer periods. Some rural points are served only by travelling banks which arrive at regular intervals for a few hours.

Museums, castles, sites. Hours vary greatly, so check with a tourist office before you set off. As a rule, sightseeing attractions are open from about 9.30 a.m. until late afternoon or early evening in summer, but not on Saturday afternoon or Sunday morning. In winter, many castles and other points of interest are closed to the public or open for limited periods. Check also for early closing days.

Offices and businesses. 9 a.m. to 5 or 5.30 p.m., Monday to Friday. Some are open on Saturday morning.

Post offices. Most post offices are open from 9 a.m. to 5.30 p.m., Monday to Friday, possibly with a noon-time closing, and from 9 a.m. to 12.30 p.m. on Saturday. Sub-post offices have half-day closing during the week, usually on Wednesday or Thursday.

116   **Pubs** are generally open from 11 a.m. to 11 p.m.

Shops. 9 a.m. to 6 p.m., Monday to Friday, 9 a.m. to 1 p.m. (if not all day) on Saturday. Bakeries, dairies and newsagents may open earlier. Most shops have an early closing day (about 1 p.m.) which varies from place to place. In many towns you'll find a "Sunday shop", perhaps a supermarket or a grocery, open for a few hours.

Tourist information offices. National and regional centres operate six or more consecutive months a year, at least from 10 a.m. to 6 p.m., Monday to Saturday, and four hours on Sunday. Local centres are open for about four months, usually from 10 a.m. to 6 p.m., Monday to Friday, and four hours on Saturday and/or Sunday.

LANGUAGE. Just because you're an English speaker, you're certainly not home Scot-free in Scotland. Gaelic and old Scottish words and phrases in everyday use can baffle English university dons. (Today just over 82,000 Scots speak Gaelic, most of them residents of the Western Isles. "Proper" English spoken with a thick Scots accent takes a good deal of getting used to. Regionalisms can be mystifying. Another problem: Scots often do not pronounce words the way you'd think they should be, from the spelling: Kircudbright is Kir*coo*bree, Culzean is Cul*lane*, Colquhoun is Co*hoon,* Culross is *Coo*rus, Menzies is *Ming*ies, Dalziell is *Dee*-ell, etc. Some words to help you along:

Scottish/Gaelic	*English*
auld lang syne	days long ago
Auld Reekie	Edinburgh (Old Smoky)
aye	yes
ben	mountain
bide a wee	wait a bit
biggin	building
bonny/bonnie	pretty
brae	hillside
bramble	blackberry
brig	bridge
burn	stream
cairn	pile of stones
ceilidh	song/story gathering
clachan	hamlet
croft	small land holding
dinna fash yersel'	don't get upset
dram	drink of Scotch
firth	estuary
ghillie	sporting attendant

117

L

glen	valley
haud yer wheesht	shut up
Hogmanay	New Year's Eve
inver	mouth of river
ken	know
kirk	church
knock	knoll
kyle	strait
lang may yer lum reek	long may your chimney smoke (long life)
lassie	girl
links	seaside (golf) course
linn	waterfall
loch	lake
mickle (as in: many a mickle maks a muckle)	small amount (little things add up to big things)
mull	promontory
provost	mayor
sett	tartan pattern
skirl	shriek of bagpipes
strath	river valley
thunderplump	thunderstorm
tolbooth	old court house/jail
wee	small
wynd	lane

LAUNDRY and DRY CLEANING. While many hotels accept laundry and dry cleaning, it's cheaper and quicker to take your clothes to the laundromats or dry-cleaning establishments you'll find in most Scottish towns. If you don't care to wait while the machines whirl, launderettes often do a "service wash", meaning you leave your laundry and pick it up within a few hours washed, dried and often folded (but not ironed). This costs a bit extra. Some dry cleaners offer an express service which should take less than half a day even at peak season. Laundromats and dry cleaners aren't usually open on Sunday; otherwise they keep normal business hours (see Hours).

LOST PROPERTY. Whatever you've lost is most likely to turn up at the police station (in Edinburgh call headquarters 311 3131 and enquire before going in person), or at the lost property offices in bus or train terminals (in Edinburgh at the bus station off St Andrew Square or at Waverley train station).

MAPS. With the exception of city and town maps given out at tourist information offices, you'll find nothing free that's very useful for touring in Scotland. But there is a wide range of maps for sale at the tourist offices, stationers and souvenir shops. Most detailed and particularly helpful for walkers are the (government-sponsored) Ordnance Survey maps. Some Scottish road maps indicate major tourist attractions. Clan maps, tartan maps, whisky maps, Burns maps, etc. are ornamental.

The Forestry Commission's map *See Your Forests, Scotland* gives a lot of information on forest walks, fishing, riding and picnicking as well as other useful facts. Long-distance walks are well covered by maps produced by the Countryside Commission.

The maps in this book were provided by Falk-Verlag.

MEDICAL CARE. Scotland, home of much pioneering work in medicine, is proud of the high standard of its health care. Foreign visitors taken ill can count on the same free medical treatment British subjects enjoy under the National Health Service, including hospitalization. Or, if you prefer, there are private doctors. Edinburgh, Glasgow, Aberdeen and Dundee have major hospitals. Tourist offices and hotels will advise about doctors, dentists and clinics in your area.

Pharmacies. In Edinburgh and a few other major centres you may find a chemist's (a drugstore——but not called that) open as late as 7.30 p.m., otherwise contact a police station for help in filling an urgent prescription. If there's a medical emergency, dial 999. Chemist on duty in Edinburgh:

Boots, 48 Shandwick Place (tel. 031-225 6757), Monday to Saturday 8.45 a.m. to 9 p.m., Sunday 11 a.m. to 4.30 p.m.

Glasgow: Boots, Union Street; tel (041) 248 7387

Hazards. During the summer, midges are a nuisance or worse, especially on Scotland's west coast. Clegs (horse flies) and tiny but devilish berry bugs also attack in warmer weather. Insect repellents aren't always effective. Chemists sell ointments for bites.

MEETING PEOPLE. In shops, restaurants, sports centres, pubs—almost anywhere—local people strike up a conversation once they find out you're a stranger. Scotland (even its cities) is a forthright and friendly place with a long tradition of hospitality which has not faded. Residents of countryside hamlets and the western islands may overwhelm you with welcome. Your bed and breakfast landlady could well invite her friends in for tea to meet you—whether or not you suggest it.

MONEY MATTERS

Currency. The monetary unit, the pound sterling (£) is divided into 100 pence (p).

Coins: 1, 2, 5, 10, 20, 50p; £1, 2

Banknotes: £5, 10, 20, 50, 100

Separate banknotes circulate in Scotland; it is best to spend them there, as they may be refused in England (except at banks). English banknotes, however, are totally interchangeable.

The pre-decimal 2-shilling coin, identical in size and value to the 10p piece, still circulates, as does the old 1-shilling coin which has the same size and value as the 5p piece. The old sixpence is now a collector's item.

Banks and currency exchange. It's best to change your foreign currency or traveller's cheques into sterling at banks (see HOURS); currency-exchange bureaus, hotels or other commercial premises rarely offer as good a rate.

Major **traveller's cheques** are widely accepted throughout Scotland. You'll need your passport when cashing them. Cheques written against bank cards are cashable in many banks and other Scottish establishments.

Credit cards may be used in some hotels, restaurants, petrol stations and shops—signs are usually displayed indicating which are accepted.

Value Added Tax. As Britain is a member of the Common Market, practically all merchandise and services are now subject to a 15% sales tax (VAT). Foreign visitors may escape this tax on certain conditions, but note that the scheme is operated only by certain large stores, small quality stores and specialist shops and, except in the case of large purchases, is hardly worth the trouble. Here's how to proceed: 1) have the purchase shipped directly to your home address; 2) ask the shop to forward items to your port of embarkation (not applicable if you're leaving by air); or 3) take the goods and a detailed customs form from the store along with you for presentation to the customs officer when leaving the country; the tax will be refunded to you in due course. Visitors from EEC countries should present the form to their home customs, who will insert the local VAT rate for those goods. This form should be mailed back to the store where the purchase was made to obtain the refund. Quite a procedure!

NEWSPAPERS and MAGAZINES*. In addition to British national newspapers, there are several Scottish daily papers. In the major centres and at airports you'll find the *International Herald Tribune,* edited in Paris, as well as American weekly news magazines.

PHOTOGRAPHY. You may be forbidden to photograph, at least with flash, certain treasured possessions in Scottish castles, museums and galleries. Otherwise, you should encounter no problem shooting in Scotland—except the weather. Well-known brands of film are sold at chemists', souvenir shops, department stores and stationers'.

POLICE. You don't often see any of Scotland's 13,000 regular police, but when you need them you'll find they're extremely helpful and polite. As in England, Scottish police are normally unarmed. The emergency telephone number of police is 999 all over the country.
Police headquarters: Edinburgh (031) 311 3131
                              Glasgow   (041) 204 2626

Traffic wardens also function in Scotland and seem to be pitiless about ticketing any car for a parking violation.

PUBLIC HOLIDAYS. Bank holidays in Scotland tend to be observed only by banks and are not always general closing days for offices and shops. Many towns have their own public and commercial holidays, usually on Mondays, when most or all work stops. The Scottish Tourist Board publishes an annual list of local and national holidays, and the following chart will give you an idea of certain fixed holidays. Remember that if one of these falls on a Saturday or Sunday, the usual practice is to take the following Monday off.

January 1*	New Year's Day
January 2*	Bank holiday
December 25*	Christmas Day
December 26*	Boxing Day
Movable dates:	
March or April	Good Friday or Easter Monday
May	Spring bank holidays
August	Summer bank holiday

* general holidays

P **PUBLIC TRANSPORT***. Scotland's extensive public transport network—buses, trains and ferries—can be of great use to tourists. If you're touring the north without a car, buying a *Travelpass* (valid March 1–October 31) enables you to ride on most of the coaches, trains and ferries operating within the Highlands and islands at important savings. Free maps, schedules and brochures describing scores of bus and train excursions are available at tourist bureaus and transport terminals. *Brit Rail Pass* permits unlimited railway travel throughout Great Britain during 8, 15, 22 days or 1 month. It must be bought outside Great Britain. Children from 3 to 13 pay half price. *Brit Rail Youth Pass* is for young people (16 to 26 years of age).

There are also money-saving excursions, weekend and island-to-island ferry schemes. On western islands you can take postal buses which are scheduled to link up with ferry services.

Edinburgh's maroon-and-white **city buses** and Glasgow's orange double-deckers cover all metropolitan districts. Modern **long-distance coaches** travel between major Scottish centres in not much more time than a car. Bus from Edinburgh to Inverness, 159 miles, takes about 5½ hours; Glasgow to Oban, 93 miles, about 4 hours.

Train services include the Inter-City train with principal routes from London to Glasgow (4½ hours) and to Edinburgh (5 hours); there are day and night trains which are very fast. Routes continue on to Perth, Dundee, Aberdeen and Inverness and there are smaller secondary lines.

For those who want to put their car on a train from London or other ports, there are motor-rail terminals in Aberdeen, Edinburgh, Inverness, Perth and Stirling.

Ferry services take you from the mainland to Arran and the islands further north, across the Clyde from Gourock to Dunoon and across lesser bodies of water. Booking is essential in peak season for the more popular car ferries, including those to Arran, Mull and Skye (particularly the Kyle of Lochalsh ferry). See island headings for more details.

R **RADIO and TV.** Viewers in Scotland, as in England, have the choice of two BBC television channels, without advertisements, and two independent commercial channels. They broadcast in colour from morning—one (Channel 4) until about 2 a.m., the other (S.T.V.) virtually 24 hours. By world standards, the television is very good.

In various areas, you can listen to five different BBC domestic radio stations, including Radio Scotland which is useful for local news and events. There are also two commercial radio stations beamed at the heavily populated Glasgow–Edinburgh belt. On short-wave you can hear more extensive news and commentary on BBC's unrivalled world service in English. Radio Sweden, the Voice of America, Radio Moscow and other international stations carry English programming which is easy to pick up, especially at night.

RELIGIOUS SERVICES. The Church of Scotland, which is Presbyterian, is the leading religious denomination. Roman Catholicism has a strong following in certain areas (100% on some islands) and a sixth of all schoolchildren in Scotland go to Catholic schools. You'll also find Episcopalian, Methodist, Baptist and other Christian services. There are synagogues in Glasgow, Edinburgh, Dundee, Aberdeen and Ayr.

TAXIS*. In Scotland's major centres you'll find most taxis are the squat London-style carriages where baggage goes next to the driver and you sit behind, separated from him or her by a sliding glass partition. They're usually black. A taxi's yellow "For Hire" sign is lit when it's available. You'll find taxi ranks at airports and stations. Edinburgh has a 24-hour radio taxi service (dial 031-229 5221).

There's an additional charge for luggage, and a 15% tip is customary. For certain out-of-town taxi trips from Edinburgh airport there are set rates. While you may not always be able to hire a taxi for a long-distance trip (if you do, negotiate the price before setting off), there are chauffeur-driven cars available for such excursions. Tourist information centres have details.

TIME DIFFERENCES. Scotland, like the rest of the United Kingdom, is on Greenwich Mean Time. In summer (between April and October) clocks are put forward one hour.

Summer time differences				
New York	**Edinburgh**	Jo'burg	Sydney	Auckland
7 a.m.	**noon**	1 p.m.	9 p.m.	11 p.m.

T **TIPPING.** Hotels and restaurants may add a service charge to your bill, in which case tipping is not really necessary. Otherwise, menus or bills specify "Service not included". You needn't tip in bed and breakfast houses. Cinema and theatre ushers do not expect tips. See the chart below for further guidelines.

Hotel porter, per bag	minimum 50p
Hotel maid, per week	£3–4
Waiter	round off
Lavatory attendant	10p
Taxi driver	15%
Tour guide	10%
Hairdresser	10%

TOILETS. "Public Conveniences", "WC" (for "water closet") or male and female symbols identify toilets in the centre of most Scottish towns, at air, land and sea terminals, in castles, museums, galleries, restaurants, tea rooms, department stores and other handy places. A "superloo" in a big city, for which you pay a small sum, may have showers and shaving points in addition to the usual facilities.

American euphemisms like "Powder Room" or "Rest Room" are not used here; simply ask for the toilet or lavatory (pronounced *lava*-tree).

TOURIST INFORMATION. There is probably no tourist destination in the world which produces more information for visitors than Scotland. Strategically placed throughout the Lowlands, Highlands and islands are some 140 tourist information centres, most affiliated with the Scottish Tourist Board, some with the National Trust for Scotland, the Forestry Commission or the Countryside Commission. For a complete list of their addresses, write to the headquarters of the Scottish Tourist Board at the address below. They're identified by blue and white signs with an italicized *i* (for information). You'll find printed information, some free, some for sale, covering a great number of subjects from local archaeology to zoology, and knowledgeable staff to supplement all the brochures.

In Edinburgh, take your local enquiries to the Tourist Information Centre:

Waverley Market, Princes Street, tel. 031-557 1700, or the Information and Accommodation Service at Edinburgh airport, tel. 031-333 2167.

For information on Scotland:

Scottish Travel Centre, South St. Andrew Street, Edinburgh (personal callers only).

The national headquarters of the Scottish Tourist Board (STB) is located at

23 Ravelston Terrace, Edinburgh EH4 3EU; tel. 031-332 2433 (written and telephone enquiries only).

The British Tourist Authority (BTA) offices in various countries will provide you with information before leaving home:

Australia: 171 Clarence St., Sydney NSW 2000; tel. 298-627.

Canada: Suite 600, 94 Cumberland Street, Toronto, Ont. M5R 3N3; tel. (416) 925-6326.

England: Scottish Tourist Board, 19 Cockspur Street, London SW1Y 5BL; tel. (01) 930 8661.

U.S.A.: John Hancock Center (Suite 3320), 875 North Michigan Avenue, Chicago, IL 60611; tel. (312) 787-0490.
Cedar Maple Plaza (Suite 210), 2305 Cedar Springs Road, Dallas, TX 75201; tel. (214) 720 4040.
World Trade Center (Suite 450), 350 South Figueroa Street, Los Angeles, CA 90071; tel. (213) 628 3525.
3rd Floor, 40 West 57th Street, New York, NY 10019; tel. (212) 581-4700.

WATER. Rare indeed is the Scot who isn't absolutely convinced that what comes from his streams, lochs, springs and reservoirs is the finest and purest water on earth. Its properties, which start to seem magical in the telling around the Spey Valley, are essential in the distilling of that even more treasured "water of life", whisky. Bottled mineral water, though never inexpensive, is available at a limited number of restaurants and shops. Scottish and French brands are most common.

Index

An asterisk (*) next to a page number indicates a map reference. For index to Practical Information, see inside front cover.